PRACTICE MAKES PERFECT

Preparation for
State Reading
Assessments

LEVEL 11

PRESTWICK HOUSE
INCORPORATED

P.O. Box 658 • Clayton, Delaware 19938

Senior Editor: Paul Moliken

Authors: Katie Mitchell and William McMahon

Editor: Darlene Gilmore

Cover Design: Larry Knox

Production: Jeremy Clark

PRESTWICK HOUSE, INC.

P.O. Box 658 • Clayton, Delaware 19938
Tel: 1.800.932.4593
Fax: 1.888.718.9333
Web: www.prestwickhouse.com

ISBN 978-1-935467-29-8

Preparation for
State Reading Assessments

Table of Contents

State Reading Assessments

Introduction to the Student

LEVEL 11

How to Take a Reading Comprehension Test

Taking a reading comprehension test does not have to be a stressful event. The following tips and methods can be used to make your test-taking efforts more effective and your results more accurate.

FOCUS:

When you read a comprehension passage, you should try to identify the following:

- main idea
- author's attitude or tone
- author's purpose

Many comprehension questions focus on your ability to determine what the author is trying to say and why he or she is saying it. Think about whether the author is biased: Does he or she support, criticize, or remain objective about the subject? What clues show the author's attitude?

While you read, you should imagine yourself as the test writer.

- Which pieces of information do you think are important?
- Is the passage about a person or a group of people?
- What is that person's or group's message to the world?
- What questions would you write about the passage?

When you come across a point that stands out, make a mental note of it. Ask yourself why the author included it. Information that seems to have a special purpose often shows up in the questions.

TIPS:

In order to determine an author's attitude toward the subject, look for emotionally charged words, such as *tragically, sadly, unfortunately, surprisingly, amazingly, justly,* etc. These words indicate an author's bias—whether the author sides with or against the subject of the passage. Simple words tell you a lot about the author's feelings.

Frequently, you are asked to identify the main idea of a passage. These types of questions do not always use the words *main idea*. They may ask for the most appropriate title or the statement with which the author would most likely agree or disagree. Pick the answer that is true for the entire passage. If no choice relates to the entire selection, choose the answer that is supported by most of the passage.

You will also encounter questions that ask you to define a word or find the most appropriate synonym. These questions check your ability to use context clues, not your vocabulary knowledge. Sometimes, you will find more than one seemingly correct answer, but when you look at the word as it is used in the paragraph, you can choose the best synonym for the situation.

Some questions are open-ended and require you to write an answer. You must write two-to-four complete sentences to answer these types of questions. The person who scores your answer will look for you to explain yourself, so be sure to support your opinion with details from the passage.

Finally, when it comes to taking timed tests, many people feel pressured to race through the work so that they complete all of it. Remember, though, that careful reading cannot be rushed. So, what can you do? When you cannot decide the answer to a question, skip it and come back to it after you have answered the rest of the questions for that passage. You may even find the answer when you are working on other questions. If you still cannot answer it, make your best guess and move on, rather than spend too much time trying to figure out one question, leaving yourself insufficient time to answer the rest accurately.

Some people suggest reading the questions before you read the passage so that you know what information you need. If this works for you, that is terrific! For many people, however, this uses valuable time and results in too much information to remember. This breaks their concentration, and they cannot focus on what they read. If you cannot focus on both the questions and the reading at one time, read the passage first, concentrating on what you read. If you need to look back at the passage to answer the questions, go ahead and do so. The point to be made here is that you should work in a manner that is comfortable for you. When you find a technique that works for you, use it!

REMEMBER THESE THREE EXTREMELY IMPORTANT POINTS:

1. **Read the passage and answer the questions that follow it!**
   Look for tricky words, such as *not, always, true, opposite,* etc. These words greatly affect the answer to the question.

2. **If you cannot remember what you just read, read it again, and pay attention to it!**

3. **Always read all the answer choices!**
   You may choose the wrong answer and miss the correct one entirely if you stop reading once you think you have found the answer. There may be a better choice further down the list, and you will miss it if you do not read it.

Model Passage

The following model passage demonstrates effective use of the reading tips and strategies. You will see that there are underlined words and phrases in the passage and notes in the margins. The notes in the margins refer to the underlined portions of the passage and serve as examples of the way you should think about the passage. These notes include questions you should ask yourself or comments you should make to yourself as you read.

The Railroads Connect

[1] This passage will be about the disorder of the "Wedding of the Rails" celebration.

On May 10, 1869, the Transcontinental Railroad was finally connected after years of hard work and confusion, but the celebration of the "Wedding of the Rails" was plagued by disorder and misunderstanding.[1]

[2] What are the funny errors?

[3] The points are organized. The word first tells me to look for second, etc. Look for next and finally.

[4] Wow, that is only four days before the ceremony.

[5] Wow, $400 of his own gold! Why? What kind of question could the test ask about this?

[6] I should look at the context of these boldfaced words. What do they mean?

[7] Those spikes were just dropped in the holes!

[8] This was a huge event if the telegraph was going to relay the sound.

Of course, the real story is a comedy of errors.[2] First[3] the actual location of the event was Promontory Summit, Utah, but since this was not on the map, the press reported that it occurred at Promontory Point; therefore, postcards, souvenirs, and even textbooks to this day bear the name of the incorrect location. Second, on May 4, 1869,[4] the president of the Central Pacific Railroad, Leland Stanford, revealed to his friend, David Hewes, that no commemorative item had been made for the event. Upset by this fact, Hewes attempted to have a solid gold rail made, but after failing to find someone to finance it, he had $400 worth of his own gold melted and cast[5] as the "Golden Spike," which was then engraved[6] for the occasion. Three other spikes were also made for the event. The next problem arose when the event had to be postponed because disgruntled[6] workers and poor weather conditions delayed the arrival of officials from the Union Pacific Railroad. Finally, on May 10, 1869, the officials from both the Union Pacific and the Central Pacific railroads convened[6] for the celebration. A special laurelwood railroad tie was laid in place at the junction, and the specially made spikes were dropped into pre-drilled holes. Not one of them was actually hammered into place.[7] Then, the laurelwood tie and spikes were replaced with a standard tie and regular iron spikes. The last spike and the hammer were connected to the telegraph line so that the entire nation could hear[8] the "Wedding of the

[9]The name of the event is mentioned again. This must be important.

[10]That is funny—after all of the problems, the important people who were supposed to hammer the spike could not do it.

[11]That is funny, too. I cannot believe no one showed up. It seems as if no one cared.

Rails."[9] The sound of the hammer hitting the spike would then travel across the country through the telegraph line. Leland Stanford was given the first swing, but he missed[10] the spike and hit the wooden tie. Thomas Durant, vice president of the Union Pacific Railroad, swung at the spike, but missed entirely. In the end, a railroad employee hammered in the final tie,[10] and the telegraph operator sent the message to the country: "D-O-N-E."

Not so surprisingly, when the fiftieth anniversary celebration was scheduled, not one person showed up.[11] Maybe they all went to Promontory Point.

1. **Which of the following best states the author's purpose?**
    A. to make fun of the Transcontinental Railroad
    B. to make an accurate portrayal of an important event in railroad history
    C. to explain the importance of the Golden Spike
    D. to describe how history books sometimes contain incorrect information

(B) *The author accurately describes the confusion and mishaps surrounding the "Wedding of the Rails" celebration. All other answer choices are merely supporting points in the passage.*

2. **Which of the following would be the best title for this passage?**
    A. The Golden Spike Disaster
    B. Where the Railroads Meet
    C. Leland Stanford's Spike
    D. The Wedding of the Rails

(D) *The passage is about the entire "Wedding of the Rails" ceremony. After all, the ceremony's title is mentioned twice in the passage, making it significant information and appropriate for the title. Although the event was riddled with errors, it would not be considered a disaster. Finally, the passage does not focus solely on Leland Stanford's spike or where the event occurred.*

3. Which of the following did not contribute to the confusion on May 10, 1869?
  A. the telegraph operator
  B. poor weather conditions
  C. last-minute planning
  D. uncertainty about the location

(A) *The telegraph operator does not make any errors. The poor weather postponed officials, last minute planning required a friend to donate his own gold for the commemorative spike, and uncertainty about the location led to incorrect information.*

4. As used in the passage, the word *engraved* most nearly means
  A. molded.
  B. decorated.
  C. transported.
  D. purchased.

(B) *If the spike was <u>engraved</u> for the occasion, it must have been decorated to show its commemorative purpose. <u>Molded</u> is not the answer because the passage already stated that the gold was melted and cast. Although the spike would have to be <u>transported</u>, the context is discussing the making of the spike, not the shipping of the spike. Finally, the gold was already <u>purchased</u> since it belonged to Hewes.*

5. Based on the information provided in the passage, what can you infer is the reason for David Hewes's melting his own gold to make the spike?
  A. He was angry that no one would help him.
  B. He wanted to become famous for his contribution to the Transcontinental Railroad.
  C. He could find no one willing to pay for or donate the gold.
  D. He had more gold than he needed, so he was willing to give some away.

(C) *Hewes tried to find someone to finance a rail but was unsuccessful. Had he found someone willing to pay or donate at least something, then he would not have had to use his own resources. Since he looked for someone to finance a golden rail instead of financing it himself, we can infer that he did not have an overabundance of gold. There are no clues to imply he was searching for fame. Finally, the passage states that he was upset that there was item made to commemorate the event, but no mention of his being angry at finding no one willing to help.*

6. *Answer the following question using complete sentences:*

Why does the author call the "Wedding of the Rails" a "comedy of errors"?

The event is humorous because it was a major celebration of the uniting of the country's rails, which was a massive undertaking, and almost everything that could go wrong did. Railroad officials arrived late because their workers were unhappy, the commemorative spike was not even hammered in, and a railroad employee, not any of the officials who organized the celebration, completed the actual connection of the rails. As a final taunt, no one showed up for the fiftieth anniversary celebration.

Fingerprinting

SINCE THE EARLY TWENTIETH CENTURY, fingerprinting has been regarded as an **irrefutable** method of identification by the United States government and law enforcement agencies. In England and Wales, the use of fingerprinting technology for criminal investigation dates to 1901, using theories developed by anthropologist Sir Francis Galton. Galton identified the characteristics by which individual fingerprints can be distinguished; these characteristics are frequently referred to as Galton's Details, and this method of interpretation is still in use today.

The scientific basis for fingerprinting is founded on three basic tenets: first, that the ridge arrangement on every finger of every person is unique to that person; second, that the ridge arrangement remains unchanged during a person's entire lifetime; and third, that the pattern is unable to be removed. Until recently, these facts seemed to point to an unshakeable method for identifying any individual.

Over the last two decades, however, some high profile cases have highlighted possible flaws in this method of investigation. One of the most notable was that of the Madrid bombing in 2004; Brandon Mayfield, a U.S. citizen and a lawyer, was accused of being a participant in the terrorist attack on the Spanish city's commuter train system, based on fingerprints at the scene, which were subsequently examined by the FBI, using an automated, computerized matching system. While the FBI termed the results "incontrovertible," the Spanish National Police were unconvinced. Two weeks later, the Spanish force identified another suspect; the FBI was forced to admit its error.

More recently, in Philadelphia, a federal judge named Louis H. Pollak issued a ruling questioning the soundness of fingerprinting evidence. While his ruling pertains only to a specific case related to a drug and murder charge, it could easily resonate in future trials. Lawyers for the defense in the case sought to have fingerprint evidence blocked; Pollak overruled the objection and allowed the evidence to be seen by the jury, but the judge would not permit experts to testify that the prints found at the scene matched the defendant's prints, which brought into question the techniques inherent in fingerprint matching. Whether other judges begin to echo Pollak's skepticism, and whether this previously unquestioned investigative technique fades in its usefulness to law enforcement, remains an open question.

●

QUESTIONS

1. Why do you think the author wrote this passage?
  A. to show that fingerprinting may be a flawed method for investigating a crime
  B. to tell the history of fingerprinting
  C. to illustrate how the use and interpretation of fingerprinting evidence may be evolving in the courtroom
  D. to show that law enforcement can make mistakes

2. Sir Francis Galton was important to the development of fingerprint technology
  A. because he showed how to interpret fingerprints in order to make a match.
  B. because he proved that no two individuals have the same fingerprints.
  C. because his theory still proves the relevance of fingerprinting.
  D. because no one has disproved his theory.

3. Louis H. Pollak contributed to the controversy surrounding fingerprint science by
  A. refusing the government lawyer's objection.
  B. refusing to allow experts in fingerprinting to testify in the case.
  C. stating that fingerprinting did not have sufficient scientific grounding.
  D. keeping the defendant's lawyer from mentioning fingerprinting.

4. As used in the passage, the word *irrefutable* most nearly means
  A. distrusted.
  B. unable to be believed.
  C. without doubt.
  D. contrary to opinion.

5. The best title for this passage might be
  A. Fingerprinting—the Beginning of Forensic Science.
  B. Fingerprint Analysis: Sound or Flawed Science?
  C. How Fingerprinting Changed Crime Fighting.
  D. Judge Pollak Confounds the Experts.

6. *Answer the following question using complete sentences:*
  Should fingerprint analysis be admissible in court or should it be excluded from cases? Why or why not?

Climate Change

CLIMATE CHANGE IS A GROWING concern in the world and one that draws a great deal of scientific **scrutiny**. Since the dawn of the Industrial Revolution and because of various modern technological advances, more and more fossil fuels—coal and oil primarily—are being burned and their emissions released into the atmosphere, resulting in an increase in the so-called "greenhouse gases" that are naturally present in Earth's atmosphere. The term "greenhouse gas" indicates that, over time, these gases can have the effect of making a planet's atmosphere similar to a hot greenhouse. The two main culprits that are causing the earth to warm are carbon dioxide (CO_2) and methane, both of which are by-products of burning fossil fuels.

Scientists assert that most of the recent warming is the fault of human beings and their heavy use of these fossil fuels, which power our cars, warm our homes, and run factories. The burning of fossil fuels releases huge amounts of carbon dioxide into the atmosphere. One barrel of oil contains about 55 gallons of fuel, and when that is burned in an internal combustion engine, nearly 260 pounds of carbon dioxide are sent into the atmosphere. If this gas dissipated quickly, there would be no concern over global climate change, but CO_2 does not act this way; instead, this greenhouse gas stays in the air for over 100 years.

While no one knows for certain how much the earth will warm, or how fast, experts believe that continued warming will damage Earth's environment, including rising sea levels, increased tropical storms, changing weather patterns, and glacial melting, which would alter the salinity of the world's oceans. Extra carbon dioxide in the ocean converts to carbonic acid, which can damage coral reefs, and continuing this process eventually may make reefs unsuitable for certain species.

Still, one might think, "Well, this does not affect me." Unfortunately, climate change can negatively affect the health and well-being of humans, too. Warming can allow the microbes that cause contagious diseases like malaria, pneumonia, or yellow fever to remain active longer than normal. Additionally, warmth allows disease-transmitting insects like mosquitoes and ticks to live longer and infect more humans. Finally, over time, climate change can get bad enough that desertification occurs—when a fertile area of land turns into desert. Eventually, there might not be enough fertile soil on which to grow crops, which would have severe consequences for a planet of nearly seven billion people.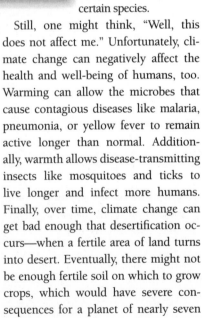

QUESTIONS

1. **As used in the passage, the word *scrutiny* most closely means**
   - **A.** criticism.
   - **B.** investigation.
   - **C.** praise.
   - **D.** confusion.

2. **The two main ideas explored in this passage are**
   - **A.** health and economy.
   - **B.** economy and environment.
   - **C.** environment and research.
   - **D.** health and environment.

3. **According to the passage, which of the following is not a way climate change could damage oceans?**
   - **A.** glacial formation
   - **B.** increased rainfall
   - **C.** reef destruction
   - **D.** increase in carbonic acid

4. **According to the passage, which of the following is a significant way climate change affects humans?**
   - **A.** It leads to contagious diseases becoming resistant to antibiotics.
   - **B.** It will cause changes in weather.
   - **C.** People will have to locate away from the coasts.
   - **D.** The earth's atmosphere may soon resemble a greenhouse.

5. **Which of the following would make the best title for the passage?**
   - **A.** Climate Change: Cause and Possible Effect
   - **B.** Protecting Our Ocean Environments
   - **C.** A Warm Planet Makes For a Sick Population
   - **D.** Reduce the Use of Fossil Fuels Now

6. ***Answer the following question using complete sentences:***
   The passage mentions "severe consequences" of desertification. What are the overall "severe consequences" of climate change?

Annie Leibovitz

ANNIE LEIBOVITZ KNEW BEFORE she enrolled at the San Francisco Art Institute that she wanted to become an artist; however, she originally thought she wanted to be a painter. This determined and talented woman discovered her true love—photography—during a family vacation and has since become the most famous female photographer in history, excluding Margaret Bourke White, the famous *Life* magazine photographer.

Born in 1949 in Connecticut to Sam and Marilyn Leibovitz, Annie moved frequently during her childhood because of her father's military career. During a summer trip to Japan with her mother, the young Leibovitz realized her talent and love for photography. Upon her return to San Francisco, she enrolled in photography classes. Just a year later, Leibovitz showed her portfolio to the editor of *Rolling Stone* magazine, Jann Wenner, who was immediately impressed with her. Her first assignment was one that quickly launched her career in photography. Her black-and-white portrait of John Lennon appeared on the cover of *Rolling Stone* in January of 1971. Just two short years later, she became the magazine's chief photographer.

Not only did Leibovitz's career take off at lightning speed, but she also had to stay abreast of new photographic technologies. Trained only in black-and-white photography, Leibovitz had to teach herself how to shoot in color.

She also knew very little about lighting. Still, her limited knowledge did not impede her success—her talent and determination were enough to ensure it.

Leibovitz photographed hundreds of famous musicians, actors, and politicians, among others, including people as **diverse** as Bob Dylan, Robin Williams, and Bill Clinton. Her photos have graced the pages of *Rolling Stone*, *Vogue*, *Vanity Fair*, and *The New Yorker* and appeared in numerous advertising campaigns, making her pictures recognizable by Americans of all ages and backgrounds, as well as by people from all across the globe.

Annie Leibovitz is a highly acclaimed and decorated photographer. Two of her photographs won first and second place as the American Society of Magazine Editors' Top 40 Magazine Covers of the Last 40 Years. One of them featured John Lennon and Yoko Ono, taken just hours before Lennon's murder; the other was a tasteful nude shot of actress Demi Moore, who was nine months pregnant. Additionally, Leibovitz's first museum exhibit, entitled *Photographs: Annie Leibovitz 1970-1990*, circled the globe for six years. She was the first female photographer to be featured at the National Portrait Gallery in Washington, D.C., and the Library of Congress named her a living legend. In the past twenty years, Leibovitz has also published several books of her amazing photographs. ●

QUESTIONS

1. Why do you think the author wrote this passage?
- **A.** to explain why Annie Leibovitz's work is famous
- **B.** to chronicle the talent and determination of Annie Leibovitz
- **C.** to compare Annie Leibovitz to other photographers of her time
- **D.** to give a brief history of black-and-white photography

2. As used in the passage, the word *diverse* most nearly means
- **A.** different.
- **B.** famous.
- **C.** smart.
- **D.** photogenic.

3. Which of the following statements about Annie Leibovitz is true, according to the passage?
- **A.** She knew as a child that she wanted to be a photographer.
- **B.** She won the Pulitzer Prize for her photograph of John Lennon and Yoko Ono.
- **C.** She is a Library of Congress living legend.
- **D.** She attended art school in Los Angeles.

4. Which of the following would make the best title for this passage?
- **A.** Annie Leibovitz: A Pioneer in the Field of Photography
- **B.** *Rolling Stone* magazine's Most Famous Photos
- **C.** Annie Leibovitz: A Fast Ride to the Top
- **D.** Photography: 1970 to Present

5. According to the passage, which of the following words does not describe Annie Leibovitz?
- **A.** intelligent
- **B.** creative
- **C.** determined
- **D.** boastful

6. *Answer the following question using complete sentences:*
Given Leibovitz's accomplishments at such a young age, what one word would you use to describe her, and why?

Avalanches

AVALANCHES CAUSE FEWER fatalities than most other natural disasters like earthquakes or typhoons, primarily because avalanches occur in desolate mountain areas or those inhabited by very few people. However, being caught in an avalanche is extremely dangerous and can easily turn fatal. Knowing how avalanches form can help you recognize the warning signs of one and get out of its path.

Several conditions can cause an avalanche, and different combinations of conditions affect its severity. Weather is a dominant factor. If it has snowed in the last 24 hours, an avalanche is more likely to occur. Any amount more than a foot of new snow can cause a slab of snow to loosen, detach, and slide down the slope, especially if the new snow does not sufficiently **adhere** to the existing snow. Temperature and wind are two components of weather that can alter the likelihood of an avalanche. Significant temperature increases can cause the topmost layers of snow to melt, which weakens the snowpack underneath, that had previously been stable. If new snow falls on that weakened layer, an avalanche can occur. Wind might not seem like a risk factor, especially when you consider that packed snow should be immovable and is very heavy—weighing about 30 pounds per every cubic foot. But wind causes many avalanches across the world. It usually blows up one side of a mountain and down the other, taking snow with it, and, as a result, the amount of snow on the sides of mountains is uneven, and the formations caused by the blown snow are highly irregular. Consequently, the wind-blown side is prone to avalanche.

Another factor is the condition of the actual snow that has fallen over the course of a season, which is called the snowpack. No one can view the many layers of snow that have accumulated all season and see a weak spot. Frequent melting and re-freezing can strengthen the snowpack, but it can also create a slippery surface that new snow can slide down, frequently at speeds that reach 200 mph. Finally, the angle of the slope on a mountain can greatly increase the chances of avalanche.

For hikers, snowmobilers, or skiers, being aware of recent weather, the condition of the snowpack, and the direction of the slope can help avoid being caught in a deadly avalanche. ◗

QUESTIONS

1. **Based on the facts in the article, what is the most likely reason the author wrote this passage?**
   A. to explain the different types of avalanches
   B. to show the most avalanche-prone areas of the world
   C. to convey statistics about avalanches
   D. to explain the conditions that may cause an avalanche

2. **Which of the following would be the best title for this passage?**
   A. Understanding the Avalanche
   B. The Most Common Types of Avalanches
   C. Avalanches: Silent Killers
   D. Avalanches: Power Unleashed

3. **As used in the passage, the word *adhere* most closely means**
   A. attach.
   B. pile on.
   C. go.
   D. rise.

4. **According to the passage, which of the following is not a condition that can cause an avalanche?**
   A. temperature
   B. melting
   C. recent snow
   D. number of layers

5. **According to the passage, why is wind a contributing factor in avalanche formation?**
   A. Heavy wind can loosen snow and make it slide.
   B. A lack of wind can prevent the snowpack from solidifying, causing an avalanche.
   C. Wind causes snow to deposit unevenly on the sides of mountains.
   D. Snowdrifts caused by wind are unstable.

6. *Answer the following question using complete sentences:*
   Using the facts in the passage, write a summary of how to avoid being caught in an avalanche.

The First Modern Olympics

RECORDED HISTORY PLACES the first ancient Olympics as having taken place in 776 BC, in Olympia, Greece. The games were held every four years, until 393 AD—nearly 1,100 years—when Emperor Theodosius I, a Christian, abolished them because of what he believed were pagan influences. Serious modern interest in reviving the games had begun when Greece won independence from the Ottoman Empire in 1821, and in 1859, a Greek-Romanian philanthropist named Evangelis Zappas sponsored what he called "Olympics" in an Athens city square. This was a local event, with athletes from only Greece and the Ottoman Empire competing. Zappas then funded the restoration of the Panathenaic Stadium, which hosted games in 1870 and 1875. Meanwhile, in Shropshire, England, Dr. William Penny Brooks had founded the Wenlock Olympian Games, an annual event that is still held today; again, this was a local event, with British athletes the only competitors.

However, the true beginning of a modern global Olympics was in 1894, when Baron Pierre de Coubertin hosted a congress that would eventually become the International Olympic Committee (IOC). While speaking to representatives of sports societies from eleven countries, including Greece, England, Germany, and the United States, Coubertin, a French aristocrat and avid athletic enthusiast, proposed an international event. He also proposed Paris as host city, and 1900 as the target date for the first Olympiad, to coincide with the upcoming Universal Exposition. Coubertin was turned down by the committee on both points; it was feared that too long a delay in launching the games would result in **flagging** public interest and fewer attendees and that the most appropriate site for the games would be in Greece—Athens, in fact.

However, Coubertin did succeed in putting forward his philosophy of what the games should be: a competition for amateur rather than professional athletes, but open to all competitors, unlike those in England, which excluded the working class. Coubertin's congress would go on to decree that the games be held every four years and feature modern rather than ancient sports. There would be complications and diplomatic challenges yet to be met, but Coubertin's dream of an international sporting event would actually be realized in the summer of 1896, with the first modern Summer Olympics. ●

QUESTIONS

1. What was probably the author's primary purpose in writing this passage?

    A. to make a tribute to Baron Pierre de Coubertin

    B. to show the beginning of the International Olympic Committee

    C. to explain how the modern Olympic Games were launched

    D. to illustrate the importance of amateur athletic competition

2. Based on the passage, which of the following is true?

    A. Evangelis Zappas sponsored the first modern Olympic Games.

    B. The modern Olympics are based on the same sports as in ancient Greece.

    C. Pierre de Coubertin founded the first Olympic Games in 1896.

    D. Coubertin helped in the foundation of the modern Olympics.

3. Based on the passage, which of the following is false?

    A. Pierre de Coubertin began what would ultimately be the IOC.

    B. The first international Olympics were held in Athens.

    C. The first Olympics were held in Olympia.

    D. Coubertin's congress refused all of his suggestions.

4. What was most important to Coubertin about founding the new games?

    A. that they be held in Paris, in time for the Exposition

    B. that the games would be held every four years

    C. that only amateur athletes be allowed to compete

    D. that ancient sports be included in the games

5. As used in the passage, the word *flagging* most nearly means

    A. increasing.

    B. dwindling.

    C. substantial.

    D. inappropriate.

6. *Answer the following question using complete sentences:*

Based on information in the passage, support or refute the following: Without the guidance and vision of Pierre de Coubertin, the Olympic Games would not have been re-established for the modern world.

Einstein and Relativity

In 1919, A SOLAR ECLIPSE made Albert Einstein the most famous scientist on the planet.

Years earlier, Einstein had pondered the theories of Isaac Newton, most especially the theory of gravity. Newton had first theorized that what made an apple fall from a tree to the ground was the same force that made the earth, and the rest of the solar system, revolve around the sun. His theories and equations, two centuries old, still accurately traced the movement of the planets; however, Newton had never been able to explain how or why gravity worked the way it did. Einstein proposed his Theory of Special Relativity in 1905, in a paper titled, "On the Electrodynamics of Moving Bodies." Building on the observations of Galileo, he showed that the velocity of any moving mass was relative to the velocity of whatever mass it was measured against. In other, more simple terms, rather than a force, as Newton had assumed, gravity is the effect of mass on space.

The most significant aspect of Einstein's work was his proof that space and time, two essential elements of physics, were not absolutely fixed and

non-variable, but were **mutable**. He theorized correctly that the only absolute in physics was the speed of light—which was a constant that nothing could exceed. This was a new way of looking at the physical world and the universe. Einstein's Theory of General Relativity, therefore, opened the door to a new understanding how the universe works.

Einstein was building on scientific observations not only of Galileo and Newton, but also of many others since; nevertheless, only Einstein was able to present and codify these observations into a cohesive, provable theory that would lead to technological and scientific advances over the course of the next century.

The solar eclipse of 1919 was the first accepted proof of Einstein's idea of relativity, which stated that the light of stars close to the sun would bend in response to its gravity. The effect is visible only during an eclipse. At all other times, light will be obscured by the brightness of the sun. When photographs of the eclipse were published, showing that the theory was absolutely correct, Einstein was heralded for his work. ●

QUESTIONS

1. How do you assess the level of scientific knowledge communicated in the passage?

    A. It is an in-depth account of Einstein, his theories, and his effect on physics.

    B. It is a basic, but fairly complete outline of the Theory of Relativity.

    C. It is a readily understood description of the distinctions between Newton and Einstein.

    D. It is superficial and incomplete, displaying a limited proficiency in science.

2. According to the second paragraph, Einstein and Newton differed in their theory of gravity because

    A. Newton saw time and space as absolute, and Einstein did not.

    B. Newton believed gravity was a force, and Einstein did not.

    C. Newton had a completely different perception of mass.

    D. Newton believed gravitational force moved the planets.

3. As used in the passage, the word *mutable* means

    A. fixable.

    B. reliable.

    C. changeable.

    D. measurable.

4. According to the passage, Albert Einstein is deservedly famous because

    A. he independently conceived of the Theory of General Relativity.

    B. he recognized that the universe differed from Newton's theories.

    C. he channeled the work of previous scientists into a cogent theory.

    D. the solar eclipse of 1919 gave solid proof of the Theory of Relativity.

5. What would be the most appropriate title for the passage?

    A. Einstein, World's Greatest Physicist

    B. A New View of the Universe

    C. Einstein Overthrows Newton

    D. A Basic Explanation of Relativity

6. *Answer the following question using complete sentences:*

    How does the Theory of Relativity change perceptions of the physical world?

The Beginning of the Internet

THE IDEA FOR a communication network between computers was initially conceived by a scientist named J. C. R. Licklider. Licklider was employed by Bolt, Beranek and Newman (BBN), a renowned research and development company. Calling his concept an "Intergalactic Computer Network," the researcher's vision was amazingly close to what the Internet would eventually become, including point-and-click interfacing for ease, e-mail for communications, e-commerce for profitability, digital **repositories** for conservation, and software for upgradability.

In 1960, writing a widely noted paper titled *Man-Computer Symbiosis*, he made the case for a user-friendly computer networking system that could be used for communication. The word *symbiosis* refers to a mutually beneficial system, but how the connections would benefit a machine was left unstated. Licklider was soon approached by the Department of Defense to work as head of the Behavioral Sciences and Command and Control programs at the Advanced Research Projects Agency—ARPA. Recruiting fellow computer scientists Robert W. Taylor and Ivan Sutherland to join the project, Licklider provided the conceptual outline—most researchers consider him "an idea man"—while putting his team members to work on the technology, and in 1962, introduced the notion of a "global computer network."

Licklider left ARPA to work at MIT, but Taylor continued his work, and eventually designed a system known as ARPAnet, the true precursor of the modern Internet. BBN Technologies received the development contract, and produced the computers and network, closely following Taylor's plans. The computers were called Interface Message Processors (IMPs), and functioned as gateways, joined by modems connected to telecommunication lines. The system functioned by employing *packet-switching networks*, in which data is broken into small packets, transmitted, and then reassembled at various destinations.

ARPAnet went live on October 29, 1969; the network consisted of four IMPs, at the University of California Los Angeles, the Stanford Research Center, the University of California Santa Barbara, and the University of Utah. The first message, sent by student Charley Kline from UCLA, was "login"; interestingly, only the letters "L" and "O" were transmitted before the entire system crashed. One hour later, the team was able to bring the system back up, and the complete "login" message was sent and received. The age of the Internet, as envisioned by Licklider, Taylor, Sutherland, and their team members, had dawned. ●

QUESTIONS

1. Which of the following best describes the author's purpose?

    A. to show how the Internet is the most important development of the last century

    B. to give a brief account of how the Internet was invented

    C. to provide a biography of J.C.R. Licklider

    D. to illustrate how challenging computer technology can be

2. Based on the passage, which of the following is true?

    A. The Internet was the sole invention of a man named J. C. R. Licklider.

    B. The Internet was initially developed for the Department of Defense.

    C. The technology that made the Internet possible was owned by BBN Technologies.

    D. Robert W. Taylor left the project before ARPAnet went live.

3. Based on the passage, which of the following statements is false?

    A. J. C. R. Licklider was more of a visionary than a technologist.

    B. A student at UCLA sent the first message on the Internet.

    C. An IMP was a method of breaking data into easily transmitted pieces.

    D. J. C. R. Licklider worked for ARPA for only part of his career.

4. What is the method ARPAnet employed for transmitting data?

    A. packet-switching networks

    B. modems

    C. logins

    D. interfacing

5. As used in the passage, the word *repositories* most nearly means

    A. back-up hard drives.

    B. storage places for data.

    C. monitors and keyboards.

    D. computer languages.

6. *Answer the following question using complete sentences:*

What role did J. C. R. Licklider play in the development of the Internet, and why was his contribution important?

Arthur Miller and the American Dream

ARTHUR MILLER, ONE OF the most important and influential playwrights of the mid-to-late twentieth century, continually tackled themes and issues central to the American **psyche** and the American Dream. He put a spotlight directly on the ethical puzzles posed by the post-World War II era of industrialization, political upheaval, and changing cultural mores. Like his contemporary, Tennessee Williams, Miller strove to reveal the dark side of the ambitious, sprawling, and often ruthless, American society he observed. He achieved his vision through characters that his audiences had thought they knew well, but they didn't know them quite as Miller portrayed them.

Growing up in New York, as a child Miller experienced both extremes of the economic divide. His father, an illiterate immigrant from Poland, became a wealthy proprietor of a large women's clothing store, until the family's prosperity ended with the stock market crash of 1929. The Millers lost virtually everything and moved from Manhattan to Gravesend, Brooklyn. As a teenager, Miller delivered bread to help his family and worked at various other low-wage jobs to pay for his college tuition. This downward mobility exposed Miller at a young age to a negative side of the American Dream—its economic system—and this understanding would guide both his plays and his politics in years to come. In fact, when he was in his thirties, Miller joined the Communist Party, although he later resigned from it.

His most famous work, *Death of a Salesman*, is a modern tragedy centered on an aging salesman named Willy Loman. Confronted with a fading future, financial setback, and disappointment in his sons and himself, he begins to succumb to the pressures. Unable to reconcile his dreams with the harsh reality of living in reduced circumstances, he commits suicide so that his family can inherit $20,000 in insurance money. In *Salesman*, Miller took the model of Greek tragedy. But he centered the play not on a king or exalted figure, but on a humble figure modern society perceived as disposable. It stands as a potent indictment of the American business ethic and a poignant elegy to those disenfranchised by the American Dream.

Miller himself stated, "The American Dream is the largely unacknowledged screen in front of which all American writing plays itself out. Whoever is writing in the United States is using the American Dream as an ironical pole of his story." ●

QUESTIONS

1. What do you think best describes the author's purpose in writing the passage?

    A. to show that Arthur Miller is arguably the most important American playwright

    B. to illustrate why *Death of a Salesman* is one of the seminal plays of the 20th Century

    C. to show the connection between Miller's political beliefs and his playwriting

    D. to illustrate one of the major thematic elements that inform Arthur Miller's plays

2. As used in the passage, the word *psyche* most nearly means

    A. moral conscience.

    B. system of honor.

    C. illusions and delusions.

    D. images of understanding.

3. According to the passage, *Death of a Salesman* was based on the model of Greek tragedy, but differed because

    A. it portrayed modern day issues and themes in settings audiences were familiar with.

    B. it used a common man as its protagonist, rather than a monarch or exalted figure.

    C. it offered a critique of the existing economic, political, and social systems.

    D. it was a downbeat, sad story about disenfranchised characters with little hope.

4. Miller's early life and hard economic struggle led him to

    A. become a prominent member of the Communist Party.

    B. win a scholarship to college, while also performing menial jobs.

    C. write about the inequities of American post-WWII society.

    D. use Greek tragedy as a template for all his major works.

5. Miller's quotation at the end of the passage

    A. is a fitting summation of *Death of a Salesman*.

    B. shows why Miller is a great playwright.

    C. confirms one of the author's main points.

    D. relates to the passage only in a tangential manner.

6. *Answer the following question using complete sentences:*

How did Arthur Miller raise the consciousness of his audience with *Death of a Salesman*?

Cubism

CUBISM, REGARDED BY MANY histori-ans as the most influential 20th-century **avant-garde** art movement, was developed by Pablo Picasso and Georges Braque in 1906, and remained at the forefront of artistic innovation until roughly 1920. It would encompass painting, as well as sculpture, architecture, music, and even literature, and would revolutionize the way artists perceived the world and conceived of their work. Many Cubists saw their art as being representative of the chaos and departure from the slow, tranquil existence of the 19th century.

Picasso and Braque rejected traditional illustrative techniques of painting, such as perspective, proportion, and foreshortening, and instead chose to emphasize the two dimensionality of the canvas itself, by reducing and fracturing objects into geometric forms, and reassembling them, employing multiple or even contrasting vantage points, thereby creating a new abstract form. In early Cubist works, such as Braque's *Houses at L' Estaque*, or Picasso's *The Dance of the Veils*, the subject matter remains recognizable, although it has been broken down into geometric shapes. On seeing these early works, French art critic Louis Vauxelles helped coin the term "Cubism," using the phrase "bizarre cubiques" to describe them.

Soon, however, Picasso and Braque took their experimentation to the next step, and they began abstracting their subject matter to the point of nearly abandoning any actual representational form. This period is referred to as Analytic, or Hermetic Cubism, in which figures and objects are broken down into pure geometric planes and facets, monochromatic in color—chiefly earth tones—a distinct departure from their earlier work, which had continued to employ striking colors. In 1912, Picasso began to experiment with collage, assembling cut pieces of paper into compositions, or using paper or other found objects and incorporating them into paintings. This was the beginning of Synthetic Cubism, in which Picasso and Braque completely abandoned any reference to three-dimensional space, liberating their art and pushing it toward the realm of complete abstraction.

Cubism quickly gained other adherents, notably Fernand Leger, Juan Gris, and Marcel Duchamp, all of whom created important Cubist works. It was also the first movement to consciously push art into the realm of the abstract, conceptual, and analytical; it pointed the way to Surrealism, Dadaism, Expressionism, and every other major art movement of its century. **⊙**

QUESTIONS

1. **Based on the facts in the passage, what can you infer is the best reason that the other artists mentioned in the final paragraph joined the Cubist movement?**
   A. Picasso was important to 20th-century art, so following him gave them the chance to copy the style of a master.
   B. Cubism allowed for experimentation, innovation, freedom, and individuality, all of which are essential for an artist to grow.
   C. Picasso's and Braque's work made them famous throughout all areas of the art world, and the other artists craved that.
   D. Cubism was a major departure from the art movements of the past, most of which were looked down upon by 20th-century artists.

2. **As used in the passage, the word *avant-garde* means**
   A. conceptual.
   B. experimental.
   C. marginalized.
   D. absurdist.

3. **What did Picasso and Braque first experiment with in their paintings?**
   A. emphasizing the two-dimensionality of the canvas itself
   B. using monochromatic colors rather that vibrant ones
   C. incorporating cut paper and found objects in paintings
   D. breaking subject matter down to complete abstraction

4. **According to the passage, which of the following is false?**
   A. Picasso and Braque collaborated on the development of Cubism.
   B. Hermetic Cubism further breaks objects into geometric abstractions.
   C. Art critic Louis Vauxelles helped popularize the term "Cubism."
   D. Cubism quickly reached a high point and then became outmoded.

5. **What single quality best typifies Synthetic Cubism?**
   A. use of monochromatic, earth tone colors
   B. a complete lack of three-dimensional representation
   C. representation of subject matter in geometric forms
   D. multiple, sometimes contrasting, viewpoints

6. ***Answer the following question using complete sentences:***
   How did Picasso and Braque help define what art in the 20th-century could be?

Hamlet

ONE OF SHAKESPEARE'S most famous characters, Hamlet, is also one of the least understandable, which is one reason for his enduring popularity. After all, literary mysteries are likely to remain interesting, while fictional characters that are completely understood soon fade into obscurity. Prince Hamlet of Denmark, however, remains as alive and **inscrutable** in the twenty-first century as he was in the seventeenth.

Hamlet is the son of an assassinated king who was killed by his own brother, who then married Hamlet's mother a few weeks after the funeral. The rest of the major action of the play centers around what Hamlet will do with his anger and melancholy. After speaking with his father's ghost and swearing to avenge his death, Prince Hamlet tells his friends that he may pretend to be insane. But why he puts on this "antic disposition" is left to the reader to discern. In the most famous quotation in history, Shakespeare has endowed Hamlet with a wisdom for the ages: "To be or not to be." Everyone has heard it, but what does Hamlet mean by it? Hamlet's intense love for his mother clashes with his loathing for her behavior. Is the way he acts a normal mother-child relationship, or does it have Oedipal elements in it? Hamlet has the perfect moment in which to kill his father's murderer, his uncle, but he cannot, avoiding the revenge he promised simply because the king is praying. Is that lack of action logical for someone who thinks of himself as keenly intelligent? Hamlet spurns his former love, claiming that women lack virtue and that she should be put in a "nunnery"; the fierceness with which he does this, combined with his accidental killing of her father, drives her to suicide. Yet why Hamlet does not blame himself is left unresolved. Instead, he fights with her brother in her grave, after proclaiming the intensity of his love is greater than that of "forty thousand brothers."

He is nearly thirty, yet still a student; a believer in ghosts, honesty, and religion; a clever forger, a madman, lover, and murderer; a self-doubter, loyal friend, and social critic; and a philosopher who ponders both life and death. It is no wonder that more books and scholarly papers have been written about Hamlet than about any other real or fictitious person, other than Jesus. ●

QUESTIONS

1. **According to its use in the passage, what is the best definition for *inscrutable*?**
   - **A.** troublesome
   - **B.** realistic
   - **C.** indefinable
   - **D.** complex

2. **What do you think might have been the author's purpose in the very last sentence of the article?**
   - **A.** to compare Hamlet to Jesus
   - **B.** to sum up Hamlet's mysteries
   - **C.** to prove that Hamlet is a famous character
   - **D.** to show how complicated Hamlet is

3. **From the details in the passage, you can infer that Hamlet is**
   - **A.** clever, analytical, and inconsistent.
   - **B.** angry, grieving, and fearful.
   - **C.** strong, capable, and hardhearted.
   - **D.** loyal, fair, and direct.

4. **According to the passage, Hamlet is angry with his mother**
   - **A.** over the marriage to his uncle only weeks after the funeral.
   - **B.** because he only pretends to be insane to fool the king.
   - **C.** when he understands that his father was murdered.
   - **D.** because his love for her reveals an Oedipal complex.

5. **What is the probable purpose of the long paragraph?**
   - **A.** It shows Hamlet at his best and his worst.
   - **B.** It allows the reader able to understand Hamlet's character.
   - **C.** It points out the contradictory nature of Hamlet.
   - **D.** It details why Hamlet is a popular Shakespearean character.

6. *Answer the following question using complete sentences:*
   The passage details many of Hamlet's characteristics and does not name anyone else in the play. It lists many of the things Hamlet does, how he acts, and what he believes. What might be the reasons the essay presents the material in this way?

Recycling

ALUMINUM EXISTS in **copious** quantities on Earth, but that's no reason to waste it. Aluminum, if recycled, can be used over and over again, infinitely. In fact, about two-thirds of the aluminum being used today has been in use since it was originally mined. So why do people throw away so much of the material when it's difficult to extract from the ground but easily recycled?

To reuse aluminum cans, they first go to a scrap metal processing plant, where they are shredded and crushed. In the next step, all outside decorations are removed, and then the pieces of aluminum are melted. Once the metal reaches the right temperature, it is rolled into a very large, thin sheet. Then, the sheet goes to a factory that turns it into cans or whatever other product it is designated to become— beverage containers, packaging, airplane parts, car engines, etc. This entire process from discarded to remade takes about two months.

Recycling aluminum cans has great environmental advantages. It takes ninety-five percent less energy to recycle a used aluminum can and manufacture a new one than to make a new can from the raw mineral, which, in turn, saves millions of barrels of oil a year. Recycling just one six-pack of cans saves enough energy to burn a hundred-watt light bulb for a full day, and there are approximately 3.4 million tons of cans discarded every year. If all the aluminum currently in use today were recycled, there would be no need to mine aluminum ever again. What an amazing environmental benefit!

Another advantage is economic. One can is worth about one cent, which doesn't sound like much, but more than 100,000 cans are recycled every minute in the U.S., the equivalent of a thousand dollars. A thousand dollars a minute equals more than 50 million dollars a year, so you can see that the monetary savings really add up. That's probably why aluminum can recycling makes a great fundraiser for charities. It not only helps the environment, but also benefits people in need. So the next time you consider throwing an aluminum can in the trash, remember that you're throwing away a valuable resource. Recycle that can instead. ●

QUESTIONS

1. As used in the passage, the word *copious* most nearly means

    A. rare.

    B. strong.

    C. bendable.

    D. plentiful.

2. According to the passage, which of the following statements about aluminum is false?

    A. One can is worth ten cents.

    B. Aluminum can be reused countless times.

    C. It takes about two months to recycle a batch of aluminum.

    D. Recycling aluminum could prevent any new mining of aluminum.

3. Which of the following best expresses the topic of the third paragraph?

    A. economic advantages

    B. cost of recycling

    C. environmental benefits

    D. statistics about aluminum

4. What do you think is the author's purpose in writing this passage?

    A. to encourage readers to recycle

    B. to show how costly recycling aluminum is

    C. to highlight the environmental benefits of recycling

    D. to discuss the many products made from aluminum

5. Which of the following statements would be the best choice of a thesis statement for the entire passage?

    A. Recycling aluminum has many environmental advantages, but can be costly.

    B. More aluminum must be mined in order to keep up with the demand.

    C. Recycling aluminum benefits the environment and the economy.

    D. Recycling aluminum is not the only answer to the waste problem in America.

6. *Answer the following question using complete sentences:*

According to the passage, recycling aluminum sounds like a reasonably simple process. What do you think the author would feel about mandatory recycling of aluminum? In your answer, make sure to cite information from the passage.

Billie Holiday's Song

BILLIE HOLIDAY KNEW too well how to bring personal emotion to her interpretation of a song; as a small child, she had endured not only racism, but also poverty, domestic abuse, and even rape. Her love of jazz and singing had been her survival mechanism, and before she was thirty, she had managed to climb from these most difficult circumstances to working with the greats of jazz, swing, and pop, including Count Basie, Benny Goodman, and Artie Shaw. By the 1930s, she was rapidly becoming the toast of the New York cabaret and nightclub scene. The clubs in New York, however, were all segregated except one called Café Society, and Holiday worked there frequently without incident. But when Barney Josephson, the owner of the club, showed her a song titled "Strange Fruit," it gave the singer **pause**. How would her audience react? Even at Café Society, might there be reprisals? She had never considered that a song might be dangerous. Yet she knew she had to sing it.

The song was based on a poem by a schoolteacher named Abel Meeropol, who had been both disturbed and outraged by a photograph of a 1930 lynching of two black men; he decided to write a response, which he later set to music. The odd, dreamlike, sorrowful quality of the lyrics did not mask the horror of the incident, but rather connected the listener to the tragedy in a deeper and more unexpected way. Billie Holiday read them and knew she would bring her own experience and emotion to these lyrics; her father, while not a victim of lynching, died after being denied medical treatment because he was black.

And so, Billie Holiday, or Lady Day as she was known, stepped on the stage of Café Society in 1939 and sang "Strange Fruit." Despite the stark subject matter, the audience response was immediate and overwhelmingly positive. The listeners felt the anguish she brought to the song. From that point on, at Josephson's insistence, Holiday closed all of her shows there with that specific song. Waiters also made sure the room was dead silent, while the singer stood still with only a pin spot illuminating her face as she sang.

Holiday's own record company, Columbia, deemed the subject of the song too risky, but another label, Commodore, recorded it, and it went on to become one of Lady Day's most recognized masterworks and biggest hits. ●

QUESTIONS

1. **What is the most important thing the first paragraph tells you about the rest of the passage?**
   A. She was a successful singer, who was becoming increasingly well known.
   B. She was talented enough to work with the great bandleaders of the time.
   C. She was haunted by a painful childhood and had endured racism and abuse.
   D. She was worried about how her audience would react to a song about lynching.

2. **The second paragraph principally gives information about**
   A. the background of the song "Strange Fruit."
   B. why Billie Holiday was the best artist to sing this song.
   C. the photograph that inspired Abel Meeropol's poem.
   D. the quality of the lyrics that made Holiday connect to the song.

3. **As used in the passage, the word *pause* most nearly means**
   A. hope.
   B. poetry.
   C. sadness.
   D. uncertainty.

4. **What is apparent about Barney Josephson from the third paragraph?**
   A. He knew a great song and a great performance when he heard it.
   B. He understood Billie Holiday's talent better than she did.
   C. He had a theatrical flair and knew how to present a song for best effect.
   D. He was an adept businessman and knew how to package a hit.

5. **What does Holiday's effort to get "Strange Fruit" recorded say about her?**
   A. She had a gift for knowing which song would be a popular hit.
   B. She was angry with Columbia Records for being afraid of the song's subject matter.
   C. She understood the significance of the song and wanted it to reach a broad audience.
   D. She wanted a popular hit and would do what it took to get the song recorded.

6. *Answer the following question using complete sentences:*
   How did Barney Josephson's idea for presenting "Strange Fruit" at Café Society reflect his impression of the song and Holiday?

The Founding of Alcoholics Anonymous

BILL WILSON KNEW he needed help. In the lobby of his hotel in Akron, Ohio, the bar beckoned, wearing down his resistance; his business meeting had not gone well, and drowning his sorrows in a drink was a seduction he felt unable to resist. Bill had been through medical treatments, religion, and even drug treatment in a desperate effort to remain sober, but knew only one thing could truly help him. He knew he had to talk to someone—and that someone needed to be another alcoholic.

Bill knew the value of associating with people who were dealing with alcoholism; years earlier, an old drinking buddy named Ebby Thacher had brought him to the Oxford Group, a religious movement that had helped Thacher quit drinking. After a hospital stay to dry out, followed by what he thought was a religious conversion, Bill joined the Oxford Group. While he found meetings to be helpful—he even recruited other alcoholics to join—Bill still battled the bottle. His doctor suggested that perhaps less religion and a more scientific treatment of alcoholism was needed.

And so Bill, in an Akron hotel lobby, turns away from the bar and picked up the phone.

The Oxford Group referred him to Dr. Robert Smith, a prominent surgeon, also an alcoholic. The two men spent several hours sharing their experience, pain, and struggle; each felt support from the other. Bill and Dr. Bob, along with his wife, began to attend Oxford meetings in Akron together. Dr. Bob experienced a relapse, but after thirty days of meeting with Bill, on June 10, 1935, the surgeon took his last drink and remained sober from that day forward. This date would later be celebrated as the founding date of Alcoholics Anonymous (AA).

Bill W. and Dr. Bob, as they would come to be known, began to collect, discuss, and eventually print up their method for treating alcoholism. One of the first **precepts** they adopted was the twenty-four hour concept, or "one day at a time," the notion that sobriety is more achievable when tackled as a daily, rather than lifetime, task. They also invented the first "twelve-step program," which became so successful that AA achieved rapid success, and by 1951, it had helped over 100,000 alcoholics recover. The group's success rate is unmatched by any other type of alcohol-fighting method, and many members credit AA with saving their lives. ◗

QUESTIONS

1. **As used in the passage, the word *precepts* most nearly means**
    A. theories.
    B. methods.
    C. principles.
    D. actions.

2. **What was the best help Bill W. and Dr. Bob realized they could give alcoholics?**
    A. the support of meeting with other alcoholics and sharing their experiences
    B. the twenty-four hour, or "one day at a time" method of thinking about sobriety
    C. the first "twelve-step program" to gradually treat alcoholism
    D. the realization that other forms of treatment were ineffective

3. **How would you describe the structure of the passage?**
    A. It's structured in a straightforward, chronological manner.
    B. It uses a flashback method, jumping between time periods.
    C. It has a circular structure, ending where it began.
    D. It uses a flash-forward technique, jumping forward in time.

4. **What can you infer about Bill W. and Dr. Bob?**
    A. They were always capable of helping each other fight alcoholism.
    B. They needed each other to battle their individual demons.
    C. They should have helped other people while helping themselves.
    D. They were conquering their desire for drink through friendship.

5. **What is the purpose of the third paragraph consisting of only a single sentence?**
    A. to dramatize Bill W.'s major turning point
    B. to make the reader feel Bill W.'s anguish, just for a moment
    C. It's just an effect and doesn't have an important purpose.
    D. It's a lead-in to the next part of the story.

6. *Answer the following question using complete sentences:*
    What was the greatest contribution Bill W. and Dr. Bob made to society in forming AA?

Dragonflies

WHEN YOU HEAR the terms *Emperor*, *Migrant Hawker*, *Vagrant Darter*, *Scarce Chaser*, or *Widow Skimmer*, what comes to mind? Video game characters? Famous criminals? It may come as a surprise, but each of these phrases is the name of one of the more than 400 species of dragonfly, the insect that is fascinating both as a species and as a cultural symbol.

The dragonfly is a large, fast, and predatory insect. It can grow to have a wingspan of 5-6 inches, boasting a long body, four transparent, veined wings, strong jaws, and multifaceted eyes that can move independently of each other, giving the animal nearly 360 degree vision. Impressively, some dragonflies can live longer than five years; however, the great majority of this time is spent as a nymph (an infant dragonfly) under the surface of the water. The female dragonfly lays her eggs on or near water. When they hatch, the babies live underwater, with non-functioning wings, breathing through gills and catching the larvae of other small creatures, tadpoles, or even small fish. When the nymph is ready to mature, it climbs a plant in order to get out of the water, where it begins to breathe air. When finally mature, a weak spot appears in its skeleton and cracks open. The adult dragonfly extricates itself from its old skin and flies away. Adult dragonflies usually live only four months or so and eat mosquitoes, flies, bees, ants, and butterflies. In fact, a dragonfly can consume its own weight in half an hour.

Besides having an interesting life cycle, these flying beauties also have significance in many societies. The dragonfly has long been culturally symbolic; however, attitudes and beliefs about dragonflies vary between the East and the West. Western cultures view the dragonfly ominously: It is known as the "devil's darning needle," "devil's horse," and the "troll's spindle," among other nicknames. Dragonflies often hold a position of evil in European folktales, and in the American South, the dragonfly is sometimes called a "snake doctor." Many negative ideas about these beneficial insects seem to be based strictly on the dragonfly's appearance and behavior.

Conversely, Eastern and Native American cultures celebrate dragonflies. Native American tribes see them as representations of water, speed, and healing. In Japan, they represent bravery and joy. Some cultures use dragonflies as food, such as in Indonesia, where dragonflies are trapped and then deep-fried. Japanese and Chinese herbalists sometimes use dragonflies in medicines. The Vietnamese use dragonflies' flight habits to forecast the weather.

With more awareness of dragonflies' role in helping to control mosquito larvae, though, many people are learning to respect and even admire these flying beauties. ●

QUESTIONS

1. **What purpose might the author have had in writing this passage, based on the information in it?**
   A. to provide descriptions and names of various species of dragonflies
   B. to compare dragonflies with other flying insects
   C. to explain the life cycle of the dragonfly
   D. to convey facts about the dragonfly as a species and a symbol

2. **As used in the passage, the word *ominously* most nearly means**
   A. curiously.
   B. fearfully.
   C. in a friendly manner.
   D. with reservation.

3. **The passage's reference to "devil's darning needle" and "devil's horse" makes the dragonfly sound**
   A. dangerous.
   B. evil.
   C. strange looking.
   D. ugly.

4. **The author uses the word *conversely* to show**
   A. a similarity between two ideas.
   B. a comparison of two ideas.
   C. that two ideas are identical.
   D. a difference between two ideas.

5. **Which of the following would be the best title for this passage?**
   A. The Life Cycle of the Dragonfly
   B. The Dragonfly: A Species and a Symbol
   C. The Dragonfly: Good or Evil?
   D. Dragonflies: Beauty On the Wing

6. *Answer the following question using complete sentences:*
   Using your own words, explain the life cycle of a dragonfly.

"Rhapsody in Blue"

It was 1924, and a news item came as a shock to George Gershwin, as he played billiards with his songwriter pal, while his brother Ira thumbed through the pages of the *New York Tribune*. An article titled "What Is American Music?" had caught Ira's eye. The story concerned an upcoming concert that bandleader Paul Whiteman was planning in New York. In the last paragraph, discussing the program for the concert, Whiteman was quoted as saying, "George Gershwin is at work on a jazz concerto." That was news to George, as he had no idea he was doing so.

Whiteman's band was among the most famous and popular in the country; he and Gershwin were good friends and collaborators who shared a passionate interest in jazz, swing, and show tunes. But jazz was the only serious musical **idiom**. Gershwin had discussed the possibility of his writing a jazz composition for the concert stage, but this was not the time for the composer to accept such a difficult assignment. George and Ira were, at this point, one of the most successful songwriting teams working on Broadway. They were to board a train to Boston the next morning for an out-of-town tryout of their latest musical, to open in a little more than a month. Gershwin had expressed serious reservations, but Whiteman had continued to pressure George to compose something, especially since a rival bandleader, Vincent Lopez, was planning his own concert, using Whiteman's idea of an evening of new, experimental American music presented in the same manner as a classical concert.

George called Whiteman and relented. On the train to Boston, he began to form the basic idea of the piece, originally titled "American Rhapsody." Gershwin claimed it was inspired by the rattling, mechanical noises of the train itself, which he would later say helped the music coalesce in his head: "I heard it as a sort of musical kaleidoscope of America...."

George returned to New York and immediately handed his composition to his arranger, Ferde Grofe. However, the finishing process was so rushed that the instrumentation was completed barely a week before the concert. Nevertheless, on February 12, 1924, with Gershwin himself at the piano and Whiteman conducting his band, the world heard "Rhapsody in Blue" for the first time.

When released as an album, it quickly sold a million copies and has sold well ever since. ◉

QUESTIONS

1. **What would you say is the major thrust of the first paragraph?**
    - **A.** to show how "Rhapsody in Blue" almost wasn't composed
    - **B.** to show the unlikely beginnings of "Rhapsody in Blue"
    - **C.** to show how Paul Whiteman fooled George Gershwin
    - **D.** to show how hard it was to get Gershwin to write the piece

2. **According to the passage, which of the following is false?**
    - **A.** George Gershwin completed "Rhapsody in Blue" in roughly a month's time.
    - **B.** Paul Whiteman led the band at the premiere, with Gershwin at the piano.
    - **C.** Gershwin completed the arrangements with barely a week to spare.
    - **D.** The title "Rhapsody in Blue" was suggested by an exhibit of paintings by Whistler.

3. **As used in the passage, the word *idiom* most nearly means**
    - **A.** group.
    - **B.** type.
    - **C.** expression.
    - **D.** experiment.

4. **From the passage, do you think the author enjoys "Rhapsody in Blue"?**
    - **A.** He expresses no opinion of the piece and simply relates how it was written.
    - **B.** He is enthusiastic about the piece and believes it is an important composition.
    - **C.** He is dubious about the piece and is not convinced it is musically significant.
    - **D.** He is apathetic toward the piece and does not seem especially impressed with it.

5. **According to the passage, "Rhapsody in Blue" was primarily inspired by**
    - **A.** the competition between Paul Whitman and his rival Vincent Lopez.
    - **B.** George Gershwin's ride on the train between New York and Boston.
    - **C.** a very tight deadline Gershwin had between the commission and the concert.
    - **D.** Paul Whiteman's desire to have jazz considered as serious music.

6. *Answer the following question using complete sentences:*
   Based on the passage, why was "Rhapsody in Blue" a significant moment in Gershwin's career?

Cyberbullying

SCHOOL BULLYING, A SERIOUS and complex issue for several years, has generated even more controversy with the swift changes in communication brought about by Internet and mobile device technology. No longer are students challenged only by a physical presence or threat of physical harm in their classes. The advent of cyberbullying, as it is now called, has turned the physical intimidation of the past into a dangerous electronic media phenomenon. From threatening emails and texts, to humiliating posts on social network sites, chat rooms, and forums, to compromising photos, videos, and personal data being shared electronically without permission, victims are bombarded with abuse as never before.

Statistics vary, but the numbers are alarming. Both the National Crime Prevention Center and an I-Safe.org poll indicate that over 40% of teenagers with Internet access have been the target of some form of cyberbullying. The most frequent locations where this virtual bullying takes place are social networking sites, chat rooms, e-mail, and IM systems such as texting. The problem is compounded by the relative anonymity a cyberbully enjoys in abusing a victim online, making it challenging for parents and teachers to trace the source of or other participants in the mistreatment. This anonymity presents another problem: It can make bullies out of some who would otherwise never become involved in such activity, since it doesn't involve face-to-face confrontation, and the perpetrator doesn't have to witness the reaction or consequences. In addition, cyberbullying is not restricted to school hours, but can occur any time of the night or day, most especially since many students spend considerable time online at home, for both schoolwork and entertainment.

How to deal with this growing problem has society more than a little confounded and frustrated; if a school disciplines a student for what the administration believes is cyberbullying, it runs the risk of being sued for **constraining** the student's freedom of speech. Parents and students are frequently advised not to contact authorities except in cases of repeated threats of physical attack or harm. Worst of all, victims are usually embarrassed or afraid to contact the proper authority.

There seems to be no clear-cut solution to the problem, but one thing is agreed on by experts: Communication is the best tool against cyberbullying, and it must involve students, parents, and teachers, not only to combat abuse, but also to establish ethical guidelines for online activities. ●

QUESTIONS

1. **What best states the viewpoint of the passage about the problem of cyberbullying?**
   A. It has to be dealt with swiftly and effectively, involving all parties.
   B. It is a complex problem, one that is growing, with no clear solution.
   C. It is a problem that is made worse by the anonymity of the Internet.
   D. It is a problem that is rapidly exploding across schools nationwide.

2. **Based on the passage, the biggest challenge in combating cyberbullying is**
   A. the amount of time students spend on the computer.
   B. the anonymity of the Internet and mobile devices.
   C. students get involved in bullying who wouldn't otherwise.
   D. that a school can be sued for disciplining a cyberbully.

3. **As used in the passage, the word _constraining_ most nearly means**
   A. restricting.
   B. prohibiting.
   C. neglecting.
   D. offending.

4. **Based on the passage, what can be inferred about students who normally would not be thought of as bullies sometimes engaging in cyberbullying?**
   A. They spend too much time on the Internet.
   B. They themselves have been bullied and are retaliating.
   C. They would use any method if it were anonymous.
   D. They believe that the consequences are minimal.

5. **Of the following, which is the best choice as a title for the passage?**
   A. Virtual Intimidation: Technology Abuse
   B. Cybermonsters: The Electronic Bully/Coward
   C. Cyberbullies: How Do We Stop Them?
   D. Danger Online: Kids and Electronic Media

6. *Answer the following question using complete sentences:*
   What are the factors that have led to the explosion of cyberbullying, as stated in the passage?

Gold

IT'S ONE OF THE MOST valuable metals in the world. Few people, however, have ever held any pure gold in their hands, yet it's been highly valued for thousands of years. Your rings, necklaces, chains, and bracelets are not formulated out of pure gold; all these have had some copper, zinc, or silver added. When gold ore, as the mineral is called when it is first mined, is dug out of the ground, it contains many impurities, which have to be burned away before the actual gold can be melted down and transformed into bars of solid gold. The molten gold is poured into a frame and cooled into a bar. Then, it is weighed, and a technician stamps it to state its purity. These bars, known as bullion, contain approximately 439 ounces of 24-karat gold. A karat is a measure of the purity of the gold, and 24 karat represents perfection in gold. Any other designation of karat indicates that the gold is now an alloy, a mixture of metals.

Gold has certain chemical properties that other metals do not have. For instance, despite its strength as a metal, gold is considered soft and very **malleable** by geologists and jewelers. One ounce of pure gold can be hammered down into an extremely thin layer, less than the width of a human hair that is over 300 square feet in area! This form is called gold leaf. Despite its thinness, though, it retains all the normal properties of gold. Gold can also be shaped into almost any form, either by hammering or by applying heat to it.

Besides being used for decoration and jewelry, the precious metal also has many uses in manufacturing. It is mandatory in making perfect connections for many modern electronics, from calculators to mobile phones to computers. This one-of-a-kind metal is even used in some dentistry procedures.

Gold is also one of rarest minerals in the world, which accounts for most of its value. It is usually found deep within the earth, but it's also a tiny part of natural seawater; removing it from saltwater, however, is almost impossible and extremely expensive, so nearly all gold comes from mining. If every speck of gold that is mined in a year were melted down into a cube, it would measure only 14 feet on a side. But it would weigh over 3 million pounds and be worth almost 50 billion dollars.

Gold has been highly valued for thousands of years and will probably continue to command high prices in the future. ●

QUESTIONS

1. **According to the passage, what is the main reason that gold is valued as highly as it is?**
   - **A.** Gold is very strong and can be easily shaped.
   - **B.** Gold has many uses in industry and is not just for jewelry.
   - **C.** Gold is very rare and is difficult to process.
   - **D.** Gold is extremely heavy and keeping it is expensive.

2. **Which statement best summarizes the main idea of the second paragraph?**
   - **A.** Gold is very valuable.
   - **B.** There is not a lot of gold in the world.
   - **C.** Gold is easily shaped because it is soft.
   - **D.** Gold can be found in seawater.

3. **According to the passage, which of the following statements is true?**
   - **A.** Only 24-karat gold is considered "pure."
   - **B.** Gold makes a good investment because of its strength.
   - **C.** A gold bar can contain copper or zinc.
   - **D.** Gold leaf is used in modern electronic devices.

4. **The passage covers all of the following topics in some detail except**
   - **A.** the history of gold.
   - **B.** how gold is used.
   - **C.** the worth of gold.
   - **D.** where gold is found.

5. **As used in this passage, *malleable* most likely means**
   - **A.** valuable.
   - **B.** workable.
   - **C.** colorful.
   - **D.** important.

6. ***Answer the following question using complete sentences:***
   What is the basic method for making a gold bar?

Harper Lee

NOTHING IN THE EARLY life of Harper Lee indicated future literary fame and stature. Born and raised in the small town of Monroeville, Alabama, she was a feisty tomboy, not unlike the character of Scout in her famed novel, *To Kill a Mockingbird*. An outsider, she befriended (and sometimes defended) a young, somewhat effeminate boy named Truman Capote; the two discovered a common **affinity** for reading, and, with the gift of an old typewriter from Lee's father, writing as well. Her father, a respected lawyer, in addition to being a local newspaper editor and proprietor, was the obvious inspiration for the character of Atticus Finch, and he instilled in Lee a respect both for the written word and for social justice. Growing up in Alabama, Lee witnessed the uglier aspects of racism, and experiencing bigotry also served as inspiration for her novel.

Dropping out of law school, Lee moved to New York, to pursue a career as a writer. There she reconnected with Truman Capote, flush from the success of his first published novel, *Other Voices, Other Rooms*. Struggling at a series of menial jobs, Lee also found new friends in Broadway composer Michael Martin Brown and his wife Joy, who once gave Lee a gift of what would have been her entire year's wages with a note saying, "You have one year off from your job to write whatever you please."

Lee struggled with writing the novel; initially it was more a collection of short, disorganized vignettes rather than a cohesive full-length work of fiction. Although she had Capote as a mentor, who read early drafts and gave suggestions, one night Lee became extremely frustrated with her work. Wearied by multiple drafts and endless revisions, she opened the window of her apartment and threw the entire manuscript into the snow. Immediately repentant, she then called her editor at J. P. Lippincott, who demanded she immediately retrieve the pages from the sidewalk below; Lee continued her work until it satisfied both herself and her publisher.

To Kill a Mockingbird was published to wide acclaim in 1960. Later, it won a Pulitzer Prize and was named "Best Novel of the Century" in a poll by the Library Journal, but Lee never published another book, despite a public that clamored for a sequel. ●

QUESTIONS

1. What might have been the author's purpose in writing the passage?
- **A.** to illustrate how Harper Lee's early life in Alabama inspired her novel
- **B.** to recount how *To Kill a Mockingbird* came to be written
- **C.** to show how difficult it was for Lee to write *To Kill a Mockingbird*
- **D.** to show the importance of dedication and persistence when challenged

2. As used in the passage, the word *affinity* most nearly means
- **A.** dislike.
- **B.** apathy.
- **C.** attraction.
- **D.** affirmation.

3. Harper Lee was inspired to write *To Kill a Mockingbird*
- **A.** by the gift of a year's wages from her friends Michael and Joy Brown.
- **B.** by her early years growing up in a small town in Alabama.
- **C.** by her father's gift of a typewriter when she was very young.
- **D.** by the encouragement of her editor at J.P. Lippincott.

4. What is the primary purpose of the third paragraph of the passage?
- **A.** to show how important a good editor is in the process of writing a novel
- **B.** to show how hard Harper Lee had to struggle to complete her novel
- **C.** to show that *To Kill a Mockingbird* began as messy and episodic
- **D.** to show how helpful Truman Capote was to Lee when she was struggling

5. Based on the information in the passage, which of the following statements would most likely be false?
- **A.** Harper Lee believed in social and racial equality.
- **B.** Truman Capote was a model for a character in *To Kill a Mockingbird*.
- **C.** Lee's low-paying day jobs helped her in writing her novel.
- **D.** Lee believed a sequel to *To Kill a Mockingbird* would not be as good as the original.

6. *Answer the following question using complete sentences:*
Who or what contributed the most to helping Harper Lee complete her novel, *To Kill a Mockingbird*?

The Technology of 3D Film

FILMMAKERS EXPERIMENTED with the concept of three-dimensional moving pictures as early as the 1890s; however, it was not until the 1950s that a workable technology for theatrical presentation of a 3D film was widely available. A key turning point had come nearly in 1932, when Edwin H. Land invented the Polaroid J Sheet, initially conceived as a filter to reduce glare from automobile headlights, but which Land recognized could be used in **conjunction** with stereoscopic photographs. Two images are projected onto a screen through various filters, while the viewer wears glasses coated with the Polaroid J Sheet, which manipulates light waves slightly. Therefore, each eye sees only what each filter allows, meaning both eyes see a slightly different image at the same time, and that produces the illusion of depth. The later 1930s and 1940s saw a spate of novelty short films employing the technology, but it proved expensive and unprofitable.

In the early 1950s, Hollywood studios were looking for ways to draw audiences away from the newly popular television and were willing to give 3D another chance. A man named Arch Oboler produced and directed *Bwana Devil*, the first full-length 3D movie. It used Land's earlier technology of dual projectors, polarizing filters, and special glasses. The following year saw the major studios jump on the bandwagon, releasing at least 80 full-length movies and shorts in 3D versions, including *Cat-Women of the Moon* and *Popeye, the Ace of Space*. But the technology was awkward, and audiences hated the glasses. 3D soon faded, dismissed as a fad.

In the 1980s, IMAX returned to 3D technology, incorporating its own advances in improved picture resolution and more accurate mathematical calculations in the meshing of the dual images. In 2003, James Cameron took the IMAX technology a step further with an invention called the Reality Camera System, which used HD digital video cameras, rather than film; Cameron shot *The Abyss* using this method, then further developed it for *Avatar*, which he had been planning since the mid-1990s, but had languished because the technology Cameron wanted was unavailable. The most expensive film ever made, *Avatar* was also the highest grossing of all time, proving 3D technology was no longer a novelty or fad, but a dynamic force in media and entertainment. ◗

QUESTIONS

1. What is the purpose of the first paragraph of the passage?

    A. to show how Edwin H. Land was largely responsible for the technology

    B. to give a brief history of the very beginnings of 3D film technology

    C. to give a basic, brief outline of governmental involvement in 3D filmmaking

    D. to show why the technology did not become popular until the 1950s

2. As used in the passage, the word *conjunction* most nearly means

    A. opposition.

    B. partnership.

    C. control.

    D. similarity.

3. What role did Edwin H. Land play in the development of 3D film?

    A. He invented the method of using two film projectors simultaneously.

    B. He invented the method of using polarizing glasses to view film.

    C. He invented a polarizing filter that could be used with two projectors.

    D. He invented the stereoscopic camera, which could record 3D images.

4. From the passage, what can you infer is the author's attitude toward 3D films of the 1950s?

    A. The scientific nature of the films is appealing.

    B. They seem to be ridiculous.

    C. 3D technology is unnecessary.

    D. Too many 3D films were released in 1953.

5. According to the passage, why did people stop making 3D films in the 1950s?

    A. too expensive to produce

    B. not scientifically realistic

    C. other technical innovations

    D. imperfect technology

6. *Answer the following question using complete sentences:*
What or who is most responsible for the resurgence of 3D film technology?

The Mayan Calendar

THE MAYAN CALENDAR, subject of much recent debate, serious scientific study, and foreboding among the general population, is, in fact, a complex system of calendars and almanacs developed sometime during the Mayan civilization's early history, possibly around 600 BCE; it is a significant achievement of the Maya, who were noted for their literature, astronomy, and mathematics. The calendar itself has inspired archeologists, historians, anthropologists—and, now, doomsday theorists.

In simplified terms, the Mayan Calendar is in the shape of a circle. It consists of three separate calendars; one is a religious calendar that is broken into 260 days; the second is a solar calendar that, like our own, consists of 365 days. These two parts spin, one inside the other, like gears, making religious days rotate around the solar days, indicating special significance. The third part is referred to as the "long count," which sequences the first two parts forward into the future, but only up to a specific point. The calendar projects forward only to December 21, 2012, a fact that has fueled heated speculations that the planet Earth, at least as we know it, will end on that date. The day corresponds with the winter solstice and with the astronomical fact that

the sun will be aligned with the center of the Milky Way. This alignment has given rise to speculation about shifting fields of energy, solar flares, great sunspots, and cataclysmic environmental reactions on Earth. Other doomsday scenarios for 2012 involve an asteroid colliding with our planet, nuclear war, even the return to Earth of Quetzalcoatl, the Mayan deity in the shape of a feathered serpent that is an intermediary between God and man.

One online vendor has over 750 different titles relating to the calendar. However, despite the **plethora** of books, videos, and websites proclaiming the end of days, scientists and scholars dispute this interpretation and maintain that the Maya never predicted the end of the world. Advanced though the Maya were in astronomy, experts doubt they would have been able to foretell the alignment of the sun and Milky Way, and some even doubt that the end of the calendar cycle occurs on December 21, 2012. The difficult process of matching the Mayan Calendar to our own Gregorian version may well mean the date for the end of the cycle has been miscalculated, possibly by as much as fifty to one-hundred years. Those anticipating apocalypse may well have a long wait ahead of them. ●

QUESTIONS

1. What do you think best describes the author's purpose in writing the passage?

    A. to explain how the Mayan calendar works

    B. to show how people are interpreting the Mayan Calendar

    C. to show the conflicting interpretations of the Mayan Calendar

    D. to debunk the theory of the Mayan Calendar predicting disaster

2. As used in the passage, the word *plethora* most nearly means

    A. a frequent occurrence.

    B. an odd assortment.

    C. a large number.

    D. a variety.

3. What astronomical fact about December 21, 2012, has fueled speculation?

    A. An asteroid is on a course to collide with the earth.

    B. The sun will align with the center of the Milky Way.

    C. The shift in our planetary system will cause sun flares.

    D. Shifting fields of energy from the sun will cause environmental changes.

4. From the passage, how do you think the author regards the doomsday theories?

    A. The author is skeptical, but open to alternate interpretations.

    B. The author completely embraces the doomsday scenarios.

    C. The author is completely dismissive of the doomsday theories.

    D. The author is prejudiced in favor of the scientists and scholars.

5. What is the physical structure of the Mayan Calendar, according to the passage?

    A. It is actually three calendars, each concentrically able to spin around the other.

    B. It is made of two concentrically spinning calendars and the third projecting time forward.

    C. It is similar to the solar system's concentric orbits, as is the Gregorian calendar.

    D. It is based on mathematical calculations, as well as astronomy, perfected by the Maya.

6. *Answer the following question using complete sentences:*

Based on the passage, why do you think the Mayan Calendar has fueled such horrific predictions?

Hillary Clinton

HILLARY RODHAM CLINTON, Secretary of State, former Senator from New York, and former First Lady, has been a lightning rod for criticism, notably from conservatives and Republicans, ever since she first came to prominence during the 1992 Presidential campaign of her husband, Bill Clinton. The irony that is seldom mentioned, however, is that Hillary Rodham was raised in a fiercely conservative, Republican household, and in her early years in politics, campaigned, along with her father, in the 1964 Presidential election for Barry Goldwater, the Republican candidate.

Hillary's father was a businessman, a **staunch** conservative, and a hard-line anti-Communist, and he remained so until his death in 1993; her mother, however, expressed a passionate interest in social justice, which made a deep and lasting impression on her young daughter. Hillary enrolled at Wellesley College in 1965. Majoring in political science, she initially served as president of the Young Republicans club; however, this group was more aligned with Rockefeller Republicans, which, at the time, represented the majority of the country and a more progressive, liberal side of the Party. After hearing a speech on economic and racial equality that was given by Martin Luther King, Jr.,

she began to question some of her political philosophy and resolved to find a future in some area of public service. Writing to her youth minister, Hillary described herself as "a mind conservative and a heart liberal," expressing her uncertainties about her own political sensibilities.

That ambivalence ended when she made an ideological leap and decided to support the anti-war candidacy of Eugene McCarthy in 1968. The same year, after the assassination of Martin Luther King, Jr., Hillary organized a student protest strike that lasted two days; she subsequently became president of the Wellesley College Association and was instrumental in safeguarding the college from the kind of student disruptions that were widespread at the time. She was later invited by Charles Goodell, a moderate Republican representative, to help in the presidential campaign of Nelson Rockefeller. The future Presidential candidate attended the 1968 Republican convention, but was deeply disturbed by how Richard Nixon's campaign portrayed Rockefeller and by what she perceived as subliminal racist messages at the convention. Consequently, she made a final break with the Republicans and aligned herself with the Democratic Party. **O**

QUESTIONS

1. What was the author's probable purpose in writing the passage?
   A. to show the influences that made Hillary Clinton a brilliant and successful politician
   B. to show how Republicans and Democrats both were influential in Hillary Clinton's life
   C. to illustrate what factored into Hillary Clinton's major political change of heart
   D. to relate how Hillary Clinton's life and career at Wellesley College matured her politics

2. In considering the passage, what do you think the author's attitude toward Clinton is?
   A. She betrayed her early conservative principles.
   B. She is a strong and admirable progressive political figure.
   C. She is a symbol of a compromised liberal agenda.
   D. She is the product of a contradictory upbringing.

3. As used in the passage, the word *staunch* most nearly means
   A. clever.
   B. angry.
   C. strong.
   D. classic.

4. In 1968, Hillary moved away from the Republican Party because
   A. she was disturbed by the politics she witnessed at the Republican Convention.
   B. a professor at Wellesley suggested that she needed to examine other viewpoints.
   C. she had heard Martin Luther King, Jr., speak on racism and was moved.
   D. she recognized that the progressive wing of the Republican Party was shrinking.

5. Of the following quotes from the passage, which best illustrates Hillary's political journey from Republican to Democrat?
   A. "she first came to prominence during the 1992 Presidential campaign of her husband, Bill Clinton....Hillary Clinton was raised in a fiercely conservative, Republican household."
   B. "After hearing a speech by Martin Luther King, Jr., she began to question some of her political philosophy."
   C. "That ambivalence ended when she made an ideological leap and decided to support the anti-war candidacy of Eugene McCarthy."
   D. "she made a final break with the Republicans and aligned herself with the Democratic Party."

6. *Answer the following question using complete sentences:*
   What does Hillary Clinton's journey from Republican to Democrat most illustrate about the American political culture?

Illuminating the White City

THE WORLD'S COLUMBIAN Exposition, or the Chicago World's Fair of 1893, as it was more popularly known, was a seminal event for the city of Chicago. **Ostensibly** meant as a commemoration of the 400th anniversary of Columbus's discovery of America, the exposition was coveted by every major city in the country, including New York, St. Louis, and Washington, D.C., for the prestige and economic development it promised. The choice of Chicago represented a pronounced upswing for the city, still recovering from the Great Chicago Fire more than twenty years earlier.

The grand, pristine white buildings of the central Court of Honor, designed by nearly every notable American architect of the period, gave rise to the fair's other name, the White City. It is certainly true, however, that these gleaming structures would not have sparkled quite so memorably without the scientific contribution of Nikola Tesla, an inventor and electrical engineer. Tesla was engaged in a heated competition termed the "War of the Currents" with Thomas Edison and General Electric for the contract to power the fair. Tesla had invented the AC (alternating current) form of electrical power distribution and labored furiously under the **auspices** of George Westinghouse, the founder of the Westinghouse electric company, to prove that it was a more efficient system than Edison's DC (direct current) method. This greater efficiency meant Westinghouse was able to substantially underbid General Electric for the contract. On opening day, when President Grover Cleveland pushed a button that illuminated 100,000 incandescent lamps, it was Tesla's system that made the buildings of the Court of Honor glow at night.

Tesla's triumphs at the White City did not end there, however. One of the fair's major attractions included the Electricity Building, at which Westinghouse mounted prominent displays of Tesla's phosphorescent lighting (a precursor of fluorescent lighting) and single node bulbs, and the earliest version of neon, inventions that clearly pointed the way toward modern lighting. Westinghouse also displayed examples of the company's polyphase systems, which made the transmission of power over long distances possible. Although Edison invented the light bulb, it was Niola Tesla and George Westinghouse who introduced the American public to the wonders of electricity when they lit up the White City in 1893. ◗

QUESTIONS

1. What do you think was the author's purpose in writing the passage?

  A. to explain Tesla's and Westinghouse's importance to the Chicago World's Fair

  B. to illustrate how significant the exposition was to the city of Chicago

  C. to show how Niola Tesla was a greater inventor than Thomas Edison

  D. to give a short history of the invention of electricity

2. As used in the passage, *ostensibly* most nearly means

  A. supposedly.

  B. falsely.

  C. belatedly.

  D. continuously.

3. If not to honor Columbus, why did Chicago want to host the exposition?

  A. to make everyone forget about the Great Chicago fire

  B. to look more important than New York, St. Louis, or Washington, D.C.

  C. to gain more fame, respect, and economic opportunities

  D. so President Grover Cleveland would visit on opening day

4. Nikola Tesla and Westinghouse won the contract to light the fair

  A. because they submitted their bid before Edison submitted his.

  B. because Westinghouse was able to underbid General Electric.

  C. because Edison lost the "War of the Currents."

  D. because AC current was safer to use than DC current.

5. As used in the passage, *auspices* most nearly means

  A. support.

  B. employment.

  C. instruction.

  D. protection.

6. *Answer the following question using complete sentences:*
Both Edison and Tesla made important contributions to the invention and de-
velopment of modern electricity. Was one man's work more significant than the
other's? Provide an explanation for your opinion.

I. M. Pei

BORN IN 1917 IN CANTON, China, Ieoh Ming Pei is one of the world's most respected architects. Both brilliant and creative, Pei studied architecture at the Massachusetts Institute of Technology and Harvard University. He went on to direct one of the premier architecture firms in the United States and revolutionize his field.

Pei spent his childhood in Hong Kong and Shanghai, where his father worked as a bank executive. His mother died when Pei was a young teen, leaving his father to raise their five children. The urban growth of Shanghai spawned Pei's interest in building. At age 17, Pei moved to the United States to attend college, and after his graduation, Pei became a professor at Harvard, where he taught until 1948, when he went to work at the large New York City firm, Webb and Knapp, which was conducting a search for "the greatest unknown architect in the country." About ten years later, Pei opened his own architectural design firm, called I. M. Pei and Associates.

Pei's design philosophy was to merge the modern with the traditional. His Mesa Laboratory building in Boulder Colorado, for example, is minimalist in design and unusual in shape, yet does not detract from the beauty of the natural landscape. The inverted glass pyramid he designed and installed at the Louvre adds a modern touch to the very traditional museum, but its distinct shape has become very controversial, as many Parisians feel the ultra-modern, all-glass construction looks **incongruous** next to the 17th- and 18th-century buildings. Among the firm's other noted buildings are the East Building of the National Gallery of Art in Washington, D.C., and Boston's John Hancock Tower, which is a 60-story structure encased in glass. Its parallelogram shape makes the corners appear quite sharp, and the bluish tint on the glass panes makes it seem as if the stark, modern building is part of the sky; the color also reflects the clouds and sun at various times during the day. As beautiful as the tower is, it was not without its problems. Not long after its construction, glass panes began to fall out, so Pei's firm replaced all of them—more than ten thousand—with windows of a slightly different construction, which cost nearly seven million dollars! In addition, the thinness of the building made it sway so badly that residents of its upper floors complained of motion sickness, so the firm had to reinforce the building with weights and steel bracing to ensure its safety. Still, despite all the setbacks, the tower stands as a testament to Pei's artistic vision and swift problem solving.

Throughout his career, Pei has demonstrated that a modern, stark structure can be beautiful and can accentuate traditional and natural surroundings. His signature style is recognized and appreciated around the world. ❂

QUESTIONS

1. As used in the passage, the word *incongruous* most nearly means
    A. out-of-place.
    B. beautiful.
    C. ugly and wasteful.
    D. valuable.

2. Why might the author have written this passage?
    A. to list the buildings designed by I. M. Pei
    B. to explain I. M. Pei's early influences
    C. to give examples of Pei's traditional architecture
    D. to illustrate Pei's contribution to modern architecture

3. According to the passage, Pei had to make improvements to the Hancock Tower for all the following reasons except
    A. the glass panes were falling out.
    B. the tower was unstable.
    C. it was damaged during heavy wind.
    D. the tower made people slightly ill.

4. Based on the information in the passage, which group of words best describes I. M. Pei?
    A. successful, determined, lucky
    B. creative, innovative, intelligent
    C. intelligent, arrogant, sophisticated
    D. humble, formulaic, hard-working

5. Which of the following would make the best title for this passage?
    A. I. M. Pei: A Brief History
    B. I. M. Pei: His Hancock Tower
    C. I. M. Pei: The Architectural Genius/Rebel
    D. I. M. Pei: Chinese/American Hero

6. *Answer the following question using complete sentences:*
    Pei's philosophy of blending the modern with the traditional can be applied to many areas of life. Explain at least one example of how an approach that is both modern and traditional can be beneficial.

The Hollywood Blacklist

ANTI-COMMUNIST FERVOR in the United States reached a fever pitch in 1947, when the House of Representatives Un-American Activities Committee (HUAC) began questioning prominent liberal or left-leaning Holly-wood figures about their politics and past asso-ciations. The Committee was riding the crest of a conservative obsession, begun and brought to national prominence by Senator Joseph McCar-thy: Radical screenwrit-ers, directors, and actors were producing films with Communist sen-timents and subtexts. Witnesses were called to testify not only about their own affiliations and political history, but were also required to "name names," (i.e., to reveal the names of friends and contacts they knew or suspected had Commu-nist sympathies). Of the forty-three wit-nesses called, nineteen refused to testify, and eleven of those were subpoenaed to appear before the Committee. One of them, German playwright Bertolt Brecht, changed his mind and agreed to testify; the remaining writers would become known as the Hollywood Ten.

The Hollywood Ten included screen-writers Dalton Trumbo and Ring Lard-ner, Jr., as well as noted director Edward Dmytryk. Citing their First Amendment rights, the Ten refused to answer the key question, "Are you now or have you ever been a member of the Communist Party?" This led to contempt of Congress charges against them. With political pressure on the film industry to distance itself from what was perceived as "radicalism," the presi-dent of the Motion Picture Association of America (MPAA), Eric Johnston, met with other film ex-ecutives at the Waldorf-Astoria Hotel in New York City and issued a press release that became known as the "Waldorf Statement." It stated that the Ten would be fired or suspended without pay and not allowed any assignments until they had testified to the Committee and sworn they were not Communists. The era of the Blacklist—and the "witch hunt," as HUAC's hearings were called—had dawned.

HUAC and the Blacklist would be a **singularly** destructive force, shattering lives and careers with frightful ease, dis-regard for morality, and amazing com-petence. It would continue to haunt the industry until 1960, when Kirk Douglas, a major star, declared that Dalton Trumbo's name would appear as screenwriter on the credits for the film *Spartacus*; for ten years, Trumbo had been writing under a pseudonym. Douglas's action showed that both the Blacklist and the power of rabid anti-liberals in Congress were ending. ●

QUESTIONS

1. What do you think was the author's purpose in writing this passage?
    A. to show how Communism, or even people with left-leaning tendencies, threatened the film industry in the U.S.
    B. to show how rumor mongering, misuse of power, and fear held sway in the Hollywood of the late 1940s and early 1950s
    C. to show how Dalton Trumbo overcame the Blacklist with the help of others in the film industry
    D. to show why refusing to answer HUAC's questions caused the Hollywood Ten to ruin their careers

2. As used in the passage, *singularly* means
    A. intolerably.
    B. completely.
    C. radically.
    D. uniquely.

3. The members of the Hollywood Ten were punished by HUAC primarily because
    A. they were politically liberal.
    B. they were known to be Communists.
    C. they refused to testify or name others.
    D. they made movies that were pro-Communism.

4. Based on the passage, which of the following is true?
    A. The "Waldorf Statement" was a defense of the Hollywood Ten.
    B. HUAC was dedicated to the concept of freedom of speech.
    C. Dalton Trumbo was forced to write under a different name.
    D. The "witch hunt" was another term for the Blacklist.

5. Based on the passage, which of the following is false?
    A. Dalton Trumbo was only one of the people hurt by HUAC's actions.
    B. HUAC abused its power in conducting its hearings.
    C. Kirk Douglas was a major star who stood up against the Blacklist.
    D. The Hollywood Ten finally received fair treatment in 1947.

6. *Answer the following question using complete sentences:*
    Why were the Hollywood Ten important to both filmmaking and politics?

Pitching Perfection

IN BASEBALL, TWENTY-SEVEN batters and twenty-seven straight outs rarely occurs. It seems as if there would not be a great deal of difficulty involved in accomplishing such a performance. After all, batting records abound, such as a .400 or above batting average (35 different players); getting a hit in thirty or more consecutive games (more than 50); hitting a single, double, triple, and home run in a single game (over 200).

The pitcher, though, always possesses an advantage over the hitter. First of all, it takes only three strikes to be out, but the pitcher is allowed four balls. A second reason is that the batter must hit a round ball, sometimes traveling in excess of 95 mph, with a rounded stick, and the ball must go where it can't be caught. In addition, pitchers usually have a variety of pitches they can throw in order to confuse the batter. Finally, it has been scientifically proven that a batter has between a quarter and a third of a second to actually decide to swing or not, and where to try to place the ball in the field. For comparison, the blinking of your eye lasts about a half of a second!

Baseball's most **elusive** target—"the perfect game"—has happened only eighteen times out of the more than 200,000 games played in modern Major League history. No pitcher has ever done it twice, and thirty-three seasons once elapsed between them. One of these incredible exploits took place in the World Series, and one pitcher actually pitched twelve perfect innings before giving up a hit in the thirteenth.

Imagine the horrible sensation that nine different pitchers had when they each lost a perfect game because the final batter made it to first base. Or consider the embarrassment of nine others who gave up a hit or walk to their first opponent, only to have the next twenty-seven batters make consecutive outs. Maybe even worse are the eight pitchers who would have joined the rarefied perfect game pitching stratosphere, but someone on their team spoiled it with a fielding error. In 2010, one of the most severe injustices in all of sports history occurred when an umpire, in the ninth inning of a perfect game, called a runner, who was obviously out, safe at first base.

A perfect game isn't heaven, but it's close. Close to a perfect game, though, is just devastating. ❂

QUESTIONS

1. **What two words would you use to describe the author's attitude toward his subject matter?**
   A. fair, critical
   B. statistical, straightforward
   C. reverential, callous
   D. light, admiring

2. **What do you think was the author's probable purpose for the last long paragraph?**
   A. to explain the difficulties involved in pitching a perfect game
   B. to detail how frustrating it is to just miss a perfect game
   C. to ridicule the umpire whose bad call ruined a perfect game
   D. to examine the few games that were almost perfect

3. **Which of the choices best defines *elusive*, as it is used in the passage?**
   A. difficult to understand
   B. rare, almost impossible
   C. not easily observed
   D. constantly shifting

4. **What would be the best title for a passage having the *opposite* point of view as this one?**
   A. A Perfect Game's Significance
   B. Too Many Perfect Games
   C. Hitters Dominate Baseball
   D. Statistics: Irrelevant to Baseball

5. **To best indicate the lack of perfect games in baseball, the author**
   A. points out the pitchers who have achieved one.
   B. explains that no one has ever pitched more than one.
   C. provides a historical view to back up the claims in the passage.
   D. compares the difficulties involved in hitting to those of pitching.

6. *Answer the following question using complete sentences:*
   Based on the passage, what would you say are the author's feelings about the large number of statistics that are used in baseball?

Pop Art

THE 1950S MARKED AN ERA of new wealth and optimism in Europe and America. Rapid economic growth following World War II resulted in more people buying homes, cars, and other goods, fueling a new materialism. This environment gave rise to Pop Art.

Pop Art, named for its focus on popular culture, began in the late 1950s and peaked in the 1960s with the works of artists like Roy Lichtenstein, Jasper Johns, and Andy Warhol. The movement focused heavily on consumerism. Paintings and prints during this time featured popular products and advertisements such as soup cans and Brillo pads. Popular celebrities like Elvis Presley and Marilyn Monroe also became the subjects of paintings. Even images of cultural symbols, like the American flag, were manipulated and presented in new ways, and ordinary objects like spoons and toilets became works of art.

Pop Art, therefore, was able to bridge the gap between fine art and commercial art. A rejection of abstract expressionism, Pop Art was easy to interpret; its sharp lines and lifelike images made it accessible to the masses, as well as to art critics. It featured everyday items— from soup cans to comic book characters to famous figures—that ordinary people could relate to, yet set these objects apart in a way that resonated with the art world, in general. In this way, the Pop Art movement demystified art and made art interesting and accessible to the mass public, without excluding art connoisseurs. Pop Art also elevated material possessions to a new level. After all, if a material object is the subject of a famous painting, that object must be of great value. The result was that Pop Art made a statement about the growing climate of materialism in the 50s and 60s. Another ripple of the Pop Art movement was the **advent** of graphic arts. Art no longer had to be created with a paintbrush or a lump of clay. It could come from photographs or computers.

Three artists were quite influential in the Pop Art movement. Roy Lichtenstein's abstract early work contained elements of Cubism; however, he developed an interest in consumerism while teaching at Rutgers University and helped spread the Pop Art movement. Jasper Johns moved to New York City in the early 1950s after college at the University of South Carolina and advanced the Pop Art movement with his unique works. Johns was known for taking ordinary symbols like letters and numbers and, with the help of a variety of media, giving them new meanings. The most well-known Pop Artist was Andy Warhol, who started out as a commercial artist in New York City. Warhol is credited as the first to figure out how to mass-produce his paintings using a silk-screening process. This further reflected the ideology of the movement— his works of art were no more original than the soup cans featured in his art. ◉

QUESTIONS

1. As used in the passage, the word *advent* most nearly means
    A. end.
    B. beginning.
    C. expansion.
    D. decrease.

2. Which of the following sentences best sums up the main idea of the third paragraph?
    A. Pop Art bridged the gap between fine art and commercial art.
    B. However, Pop Art also elevated material possessions to a new level.
    C. The result was that Pop Art made a statement about the growing climate of materialism in the 50s and 60s.
    D. Another ripple of the Pop Art movement was the advent of graphic arts.

3. Which of the following would make the best title for this passage?
    A. Pop Art: Just a Pop in the Art Pan
    B. Lichtenstein, Johns, and Warhol: American Masters
    C. Pop Art: A Reflection of Our Everyday World
    D. Art After World War II

4. According to the passage, Pop Art features
    A. extreme colors.
    B. an abundance of texture.
    C. common, unknown people.
    D. clear images and sharp lines.

5. Which of the following statements is false?
    A. Pop Art was a continuation of abstract expressionist art.
    B. Pop Art is easy to interpret.
    C. Pop Art reflected society's consumerism at the time.
    D. Pop Art could be mass-produced easily.

6. *Answer the following question using complete sentences:*
In what way or ways do you think Pop Art continues to influence American culture today?

The First Lady's Mission

IT SEEMS THAT EVERY First Lady of the last four decades has chosen a single cause to champion, bringing the power of celebrity and access to the media so as to focus the public's attention on a particular goal or problem. From Jacqueline Kennedy's historical renovation of the White House, to Lady Bird Johnson's beautification of America, to Laura Bush's crusade against illiteracy, the nation's First Ladies have usually helped define their roles by some manner of **advocacy**. For Michelle Obama, the fight against childhood obesity is the cause she chose to spotlight, and she set an ambitious goal—to end obesity in the nation's children within a generation.

The statistics on the problem are horrible. In the course of the last three decades, the childhood obesity rate in this country has tripled, meaning fully one in three children today is obese. The impact on the present and future health of the nation's youth will be disastrous, with increased risk for diabetes, heart disease, high blood pressure, and even cancer. There are various causes for this startling increase in the obesity rate. Decreased exercise is foremost, as kids today are more likely to be driven or bused to school than walk. A second cause is the national epidemic of inactivity, as young people are addicted to playing sedentary computer, smart phone or video games, and do not engage in physical activity. Perhaps most noteworthy, is that, because of fast food, Americans of all ages are now eating 31% more calories than thirty years ago. All these facts have conspired to severely endanger the health of future generations of Americans.

Mrs. Obama's plan confronted the crisis with a two-fold strategy. Calling her campaign "Let's Move!" she focused attention on improved nutrition at home and school, stressing the value of healthier choices, as well as the need for more exercise and physical activities. In May 2010, the First Lady stated, "For the first time, the nation will have goals, benchmarks, and measurable outcomes that will help us tackle the childhood obesity epidemic one child, one family, and one community at a time." She went on, urging all sectors to cooperate in the fight to improve young people's health. Specifically pointing to parents, schools, public officials, business leaders, and professional athletes, all of whom have an influence on children's eating habits, Mrs. Obama, like her predecessors, dedicated herself and the office of First Lady to a worthy cause. ●

QUESTIONS

1. **As used in the passage, the word** *advocacy* **most nearly means**
   - **A.** mission.
   - **B.** public support.
   - **C.** goal setting.
   - **D.** assistance.

2. **What do you think is the author's purpose in the second paragraph?**
   - **A.** to illustrate the scope of the problem of childhood obesity
   - **B.** to show why diet and exercise are necessary to children's health
   - **C.** to offer his or her opinionated views on the subject of obesity
   - **D.** to detail what is wrong with young children's habits in modern society

3. **From the passage, what do you think is the author's attitude toward Mrs. Obama?**
   - **A.** impartial and objective, without any particular opinion toward her
   - **B.** fairly positive and sincere in his attitude toward her
   - **C.** overly positive and too uncritical of her
   - **D.** skeptical of her initiative, not convinced she is sincere

4. **How well do you think the quote from Mrs. Obama in the last paragraph relates to the passage?**
   - **A.** It is on point, greatly advancing the reader's understanding of the passage.
   - **B.** It is relevant, but restates what has already been stated.
   - **C.** It is irrelevant, and doesn't contribute to the reader's understanding.
   - **D.** It gives the reader a basic idea of the strategy of Mrs. Obama's plan.

5. **What is Mrs. Obama advocating as explained by her quote and the summary of it?**
   - **A.** a substantially improved diet and exercise plan for all American families
   - **B.** a diverse, multi-pronged approach to solving childhood obesity
   - **C.** a government-sponsored plan to solve the problem of childhood obesity
   - **D.** the involvement of the private sector in solving childhood obesity

6. *Answer the following question using complete sentences:*
   What about Michelle Obama's "Let's Move!" campaign distinguished it from causes put forward by other First Ladies?

The Invention of Television

PHILO FARNSWORTH, A LARGELY self-taught American inventor, is generally credited with having invented television in 1927. In truth, however, scientists had been experimenting with various methods of transmitting images for many years before. As early as 1862, Giovanni Caselli invented the Pantelegraph, an early version of a fax machine that could transmit images over telegraph lines. In 1880, both Alexander Graham Bell and Thomas Edison were exploring the possibility of transmitting images over telephone lines, and in 1884, Paul Nipkow succeeded in sending images over wires with a technology that involved a rotating metal disc he called a "telescope." The development of the cathode ray tube, later termed a picture tube, came in 1897 from German physicist Ferdinand Braun. A cathode ray tube (or CRT) is essentially a large glass tube with a vacuum inside consisting of one or more electron guns and a phosphorescent surface on which images can be projected. This was the first fully electronic television device.

Many other inventors continued to explore and improve the imaging technology, but it was Farnsworth who discovered an actual system that made broadcast television possible. Perfecting a device known as an image dissector, a video camera-like tube that focuses an image on photosensitive material,

Farnsworth's system was unique because it involved electronic scanning of both the pickup and display devices. In 1928, Farnsworth revealed his innovation to the press; the following year, he had improved the technology to the point that the first electronic transmission of live images was possible.

Concurrently, Vladimir Zworykin, a Russian-American inventor and engineer, was working for Radio Corporation of America (RCA) on his own version of an electronic television system. Rather than depending on Farnsworth's image dissector, Zworykin employed his own device, the iconoscope, a camera tube that converted images into electrical impulses. After five years of development, in 1934, RCA demonstrated the device, and a "patent war" developed between Farnsworth and RCA, headed by the powerful David Sarnoff. The lone inventor, however, was no match for RCA, the corporate giant, neither in financial resources nor in legal power, and Farnsworth would never reap substantial monetary benefit from his invention. Sarnoff spent over $10 million in research and development of Zworykin's system, and on April 30, 1939, at the New York World's Fair, RCA, for the first time, revealed commercial television to the public, who could view Franklin Delano Roosevelt's remarks on one of the very few TV receivers in the world. ●

QUESTIONS

1. What best describes the author's purpose in writing the passage?
- **A.** to show how Philo Farnsworth was the major figure in the development of television
- **B.** to show how television was slowly but continuously being developed by many inventors
- **C.** to show how television could never have been invented if RCA hadn't been involved
- **D.** to show how Zworykin's iconoscope was superior to Farnsworth's image dissector

2. What invention first pointed the way toward television?
- **A.** Caselli's Pantelegraph machine
- **B.** Nipkow's telescope
- **C.** Bell's telephone
- **D.** Zworykin's iconoscope

3. As used in the passage, the word *concurrently* most nearly means
- **A.** with an electrical current.
- **B.** in a different place.
- **C.** at the same time.
- **D.** with great care.

4. Zworykin's invention proved to be dominant over Farnsworth's because
- **A.** it transmitted images faster.
- **B.** it transmitted better quality images.
- **C.** it was less expensive to operate.
- **D.** it had RCA's resources backing it.

5. Farnsworth's image dissector was a system unlike the others because
- **A.** it was able to scan both the pickup and display devices.
- **B.** it could project moving images, such as human beings.
- **C.** it depended on mechanical devices rather than electronic ones.
- **D.** it focused an image on photosensitive material.

6. *Answer the following question using complete sentences:*
Was Philo Farnsworth a failure or a success as an inventor?

Recession

RECESSION HAS COME to be basically defined as a cycle where Gross Domestic Product (GDP) is negative for a period of six months or longer. In fact, a number of economic indicators usually point to a recession before the onset of an actual economically defined recession, notably increased unemployment, declining wholesale and retail sales, and a destabilized housing market. The National Bureau of Economic Research (NBER), a non-profit economic research organization widely regarded as the most expert source on the subject, defines a recession as "a significant decline in economic activity spread across the country, lasting more than a few months, normally visible in real GDP growth, real personal income...and wholesale-retail sales."

The recession of 2007-2009 was largely preceded by the bursting of the "housing bubble," when housing prices, which had risen steeply and very rapidly over several years, suddenly fell. The hangover-like effects of debt from reckless lending by banks, especially on variable rate mortgages, led to the most severe banking crisis since the Great Depression of the 1930s.

Ironically, the root cause in 2007-2009 dates to the previous recession in 2001, which followed the bursting of the "dot-com bubble." To combat the economic situation, in 2003, the Federal Reserve, the country's chief banking regulator, lowered interest rates to historical levels, just 1%. The 2001 recession was thus short lived, but the loose monetary policy led to a frenzy of debt-financed consumption that brought about near-total economic collapse six years later.

Another key ingredient in the 2007-2009 failure was the lack of regulation of financial institutions, such as investment banks and hedge funds, now referred to as America's "shadow banking system." Unlike banks, however, these entities were not required to have a minimum amount of money on hand relative to what they lend and borrow. A key example was Lehman Brothers, a global financial services firm that had dealt in investment banking and management, securities, equities, and other financial products. This company, established in 1850, was forced into bankruptcy in 2008, when the perfect storm of a plunging stock market, the collapsing mortgage market, the devaluation of its credit rating, and the mass exodus of its clients spelled the end of the formerly **venerable** institution. The Lehman bankruptcy was the largest in U.S. history.

According to most economists, the potential of recession will always be present in industrialized societies, but proper responses by governments can limit economic disaster through responsible policies. ○

QUESTIONS

1. What do you think best describes the author's purpose in the second paragraph?
  A. to give a basic explanation of the recession of '07-'09
  B. to explain the U.S. monetary and financial policy of '07-'09
  C. to illustrate the severity of the crisis of '07-'09
  D. to show how housing caused the problems in '07-'09

2. According to the passage, which of the following is true about Lehman Brothers?
  A. It was largely responsible for the financial crisis of '07-'09.
  B. It acted as a symbol of financial miscalculations of '07-'09.
  C. It was less reckless than other "shadow banking" firms were in '07-'09.
  D. Its collapse was primarily unrelated to the financial crisis of '07-'09.

3. What role did the collapse of the "housing bubble" play in the recession?
  A. It prompted economic collapse because of deflating home prices.
  B. It contributed to the recession by encouraging risky lending practices.
  C. It caused recession by encouraging people to buy expensive homes.
  D. It contributed to the recession because of increased defaults on loans.

4. As used in the passage, the word *venerable* most nearly means
  A. corrupt and reviled due to illegal practices.
  B. out-of-touch and irrelevant because of changing times.
  C. respected and esteemed because of longevity.
  D. extinct and powerless because of factors beyond its control.

5. The 2001 recession led to the 2007-2009 recession by
  A. tightening credit and lending.
  B. encouraging reckless lending.
  C. deflating the housing market.
  D. regulating financial institutions.

6. *Answer the following question using complete sentences:*
  Based on the passage, what lessons can be learned from the 2007-2009 recession?

The Pacific Garbage Patches

WHEN ONE THINKS of the Pacific Ocean, the image that might be **conjured** up is one of a vast, blue ocean, fascinating marine animals, and exotic island beaches. However, something unusual floats atop the deep open waters of the Pacific Ocean—tons of primarily plastic trash. The media and scientists have estimated the size and nature of these "garbage patches," likening them to huge, floating islands of discarded waste where trash has accumulated in the ocean, posing a threat to marine life.

There are two main patches of marine debris in the Pacific: One is halfway between California and Hawaii, and the other lies off the coast of Japan. Currents and winds cause plastic garbage, which is lightweight, to accumulate. The patches are not solid islands of plastic, nor do the areas have any definite boundaries. Because the water moves, the patches constantly change shape, size, and location. Furthermore, because much of the trash is very small pieces of plastic, the patches cannot be seen by satellite and, therefore, cannot be accurately measured. Still, these huge amounts of trash in the ocean are harmful.

Not only does the trash pollute the water and the habitat for countless marine species, but it is also mistaken for food by birds, fish, and turtles. When plastic degrades, it does not break down chemically; it only breaks into smaller plastic bits, called "nurdles."

Marine animals ingest these nurdles, frequently resulting in deadly intestinal blockages and exposure to toxic chemicals, both of which usually lead to death. Other animals die when they become enmeshed in round plastic six-pack holders, in no-longer-usable fish netting, or in fishing line.

Unfortunately, efforts to clean up the vast tracts of human waste products could be nearly as harmful and extremely difficult. First of all, the size of these floating trash heaps is estimated to cover an area as small as Texas and as large as the continental U.S. Based on that alone, it would take years for a fleet of boats large enough to remove all the litter, which, in itself would add pollution to the Pacific. Another problem is that the movement of the garbage makes its exact location difficult to determine, so many parts of it would probably escape detection. Finally, scientists have not yet figured out a way to remove the trash from the water without also extracting microscopic marine life, which could permanently cripple life in that area of the ocean.

Despite the futility of the situation, a few dedicated researchers are determined to clean up the mess, even if they must remove every piece of plastic by hand. They hope that by educating the public about these potentially deadly killing fields, people will become more aware of how they dispose of trash and start doing so more responsibly. ❍

QUESTIONS

1. Why can't the garbage patches be accurately measured?
   A. Most of the trash is under water and cannot be seen.
   B. The mass of trash is so large that ordinary instruments cannot measure it.
   C. The trash is mostly fragments of plastic and can't be accurately measured.
   D. The amount of trash in the ocean constantly fluctuates.

2. As used in the passage, the word *conjured* most nearly means
   A. hoped.
   B. magically appeared.
   C. brought to mind.
   D. debated.

3. The writer's tone in the last paragraph can best be described as
   A. hopeful.
   B. desperate.
   C. informative.
   D. disappointed.

4. Why do you think the author wrote this passage?
   A. to explain the dangerous effects of chemicals found in plastic
   B. to warn people about vacationing on Maui or Fiji because of the plastic
   C. to describe various marine life in the Pacific Ocean
   D. to discuss the problems caused by trash in the ocean

5. According to the passage, which statement is false?
   A. Nurdles are tiny bits of broken plastic.
   B. Scientists recently discovered a way to clean up the trash.
   C. The trash accumulates in the ocean because it gets caught in currents.
   D. Ingesting plastic can be fatal.

6. *Answer the following question using complete sentences:*
   What attitude does the writer bring to the subject? Quote some sentences or list some ideas that led you to your conclusion.

Mies van der Rohe

In 1947, Mies van der Rohe, who was widely regarded as one of the preeminent architects of the Modernist movement, received a private commission to design and build what would become a signature building, one that would define both his design **aesthetic** as unique and offer a new direction for architecture in the twentieth century—as well as fuel debate over the nature and function of architecture itself.

An émigré from Germany who had once headed the influential Bauhaus school, Mies had fled the creative oppression of the Nazi regime in 1937 to pursue opportunity in the United States, settling in Chicago and accepting a position as head of the architecture school at the Illinois Institute of Technology. In Chicago, he met Dr. Edith Farnsworth, who was determined to commission an important piece of architecture and possessed the means to finance such a project. Farnsworth proposed a plot of land she owned southwest of Chicago as a site for a home and weekend retreat. Upon accepting the commission, Mies conceived a design that exploited the beauty of the setting fully, while defining a living space in a completely unprecedented way.

Never before had the idea of a house made primarily of glass ever been attempted; the structural challenges alone flew in the face of established building practices, and the notion of an almost completely transparent living space seemed to defy any notion of practicality. Mies, however, was undeterred and designed a home that was essentially a single room. It contained a central cylindrical core covered by two large wooden slabs, one providing the area for the kitchen and bathroom, the other a wardrobe. The remaining space was unobstructed, visible from and to the outside, and meant to be flexible in use. Much controversy resulted from the apparent lack of attention to domestic needs, specifically privacy, and conflict developed between Mies and Farnsworth over building and maintenance costs, the aforementioned lack of privacy, and the huge swarms of insects that were attracted at night by the brilliantly lit interior.

Praised in the architectural press and lionized in the decades since for its purity of design, the house never pleased its owner, who would later refer to it as "my Miesconception." It is now owned by the state of Illinois and maintained as a museum. ●

QUESTIONS

1. Why did the author write this passage?

   A. to show that modern architecture is inferior to previous styles

   B. to illustrate why Mies van der Rohe is an important architect

   C. to relate how a significant architectural landmark came into being

   D. to tell an ironic tale about the conflict between artist and sponsor

2. As used in the passage, the word *aesthetic* most nearly means

   A. pleasing to the eye.

   B. vision.

   C. method.

   D. theory or philosophy.

3. Based on the passage, which of the following is false?

   A. Mies van der Rohe was devoted to his vision of architecture.

   B. Mies van der Rohe fled Germany for America to seek opportunity.

   C. Mies van der Rohe was part of the mainstream architectural community.

   D. Mies van der Rohe is seen as an important architect of the Modernist movement.

4. According to the passage, what is the most significant aspect of the Farnsworth House?

   A. It was beautiful, but impossible for Farnsworth to live in, even as a retreat.

   B. It was innovative in the aesthetics and technology of architecture.

   C. It showcased the beauty of the natural setting surrounding it.

   D. It employed building materials that were unusual for its time.

5. Based on the passage, why was Dr. Farnsworth unhappy with Mies's design?

   A. She disliked the way it looked because it had only one room.

   B. She wanted it built facing in a different direction.

   C. Mies wouldn't take any of her suggestions into consideration.

   D. There was a lack of privacy, it was costly, and it attracted insects.

6. *Answer the following question using complete sentences:*

   Based on the article, do you think it is an architect's job to please the paying client, or to further a creative vision?

The Early Roots and Rise of Nazism

THE TWISTED CONCEPTS and mistaken beliefs that were an inherent element of Nazism did not, in fact, originate from their most prominent and infamous proponent, Adolf Hitler. Anti-Semitism, anti-Communism, along with the **veneration** and idolization of the Aryan race above all others were precepts espoused by the elitist Thule Society and Vril Society, as well as the *Deutsche Arbeiterpartei* (DAP, or German Workers' Party), the direct precursor of the National Socialist Workers' Party, or Nazi Party, as it came to be known.

The Thule Society, which called itself a "German study group," fostered the myth of the Aryan as the truest, purest German; while the members also supported this belief with a folkloric legend about a lost northern land named Ultima Thule, a kind of Olympus on Earth, their true interest was marginalizing Jews and Communists and promoting a radically racist viewpoint. It is unclear whether Hitler himself was a member, but many of his inner circle were, and the fanatical ideology obviously had an early impact on his own philosophy. The DAP, on the other hand, financially sponsored by the Thule Society, was overtly political, devoted to a fanatical German nationalism, and fixed on seizing power and influence in the government.

However, another major element contributed to the events that climaxed in the rise of Nazism: the post-World War I economic and political crisis of the Weimar Republic, the ruling body that had been established after the German defeat in the Great War. Faced with deep resentment of the Treaty of Versailles, which required Germany to pay heavy war reparations, and the hyperinflation caused by the overproduction of money to pay off debt that rendered the currency nearly worthless, the government struggled to establish stability. As an example, in 1919, it took 63 Deutschmarks to buy one U.S. dollar and by 1924, it took over *one trillion* to buy a dollar.

Nazism, meanwhile, continued to stoke the fires of National Socialism's ideological hold on its adherents and expand its base of support. The next several years marked a period of relative stability in Germany, with an improved economy, a thriving cultural scene, and less civil unrest. This came to an end, however, with the economic collapse of the Great Depression; the Weimar Republic found itself in decline, with dwindling credibility and failed economic policies. In 1933, Adolf Hitler and his National Socialist Party, on a wave of anger and fanatical nationalist fervor, were swept into power. ●

QUESTIONS

1. What was the author's main purpose in writing the passage?

    A. to show how Adolf Hitler and the Nazis seized power from the Weimar Republic

    B. to show how fanatical beliefs and economic instability set the stage for Nazism's rise

    C. to show the fallacy of the ideology of the National Socialist movement

    D. to show how the weakness of German society caused the rise of Nazism

2. How did the Thule Society substantially contribute to the rise of Nazism?

    A. by providing an ideological and mystical base for the National Socialist movement

    B. by allowing Hitler and his inner circle of associates access to their meetings

    C. by sponsoring the DAP, the precursor of the National Socialist (Nazi) Party

    D. by promoting anti-Semitism and the superiority of the Aryan race

3. As used in the passage, the word *veneration* most nearly means

    A. worship.

    B. position.

    C. decline.

    D. definition.

4. Which of the following can you logically infer from the passage?

    A. The Nazis exploited the weakness of the Weimar Republic, but couldn't assume power.

    B. Without economic and political instability, Nazism would not have ruled Germany.

    C. German governmental interference in economic matters was unnecessary.

    D. The Great Depression and hyperinflation were sufficient to bring Hitler to power.

5. Based on the passage, which would be the most appropriate title from the following?

    A. The Thule Society and the DAP: The Building Blocks of Nazism

    B. Adolf Hitler, Mysticism, and the Cult of the Aryan Nation

    C. The Perfect Storm: Fanaticism Meets Economic and Political Turmoil

    D. The Fall of The Weimar Republic and Rise of Evil in Germany

6. *Answer the following question using complete sentences:*

Based on facts stated in the passage, what was the most significant contributing factor in the rise of the Nazi Party?

The Films of Alfred Hitchcock

WITHOUT A DOUBT, Alfred Hitchcock was one of the leading film artists of the twentieth century; "Hitch" directed a body of work that, while hugely popular and commercially successful, is also a unique expression of a personal vision. That vision was frequently dark in its portrayal of human relations, psychology, and society, but it was also peppered with Hitchcock's sly humor, his elegant visual sense, and his astounding filmmaking technique.

Widely touted as "the master of suspense," Hitchcock used fear both as a subject and storytelling tool. Preferring the technique of suspense rather than shock, he believed the best method to engage an audience was to give them information the characters onscreen were unaware of, and then make the viewers agonize over the expected climax. In *Vertigo*, possibly Hitchcock's most personal film, his entire crew disagreed with his choice of letting the audience know two-thirds into the film that Judy has been masquerading as Madeleine, the woman that Scottie is obsessed with; everyone felt the revelation should be held till the final sequence as a surprise ending. But Hitchcock was resolute, preferring to increase the tension in the story, putting us on edge as we wonder what Scottie's response will be when he finds that he's been duped. This choice deepens the film, making us think more about the nature of relationships and human nature than experiencing mere sensation.

Another notable Hitchcock technique is his camera work, which is renowned both for its technical innovation and for the conscious effect it has on his audiences. Pioneering the method of point of view shots, Hitchcock makes his audience into a collective **voyeur**, seeing the secrets of the characters and unwittingly sharing their terror and moral ambiguity. Most notably in *Rear Window* and *Psycho*, the audience is made to identify with the characters, then made uncomfortable by the implications of this knowledge. Whether watching James Stewart's seemingly benign observing of the lives of his neighbors or Anthony Perkins's peering through a peephole at Janet Leigh, the audience is first drawn in, then made to consider the darker side of its own nature. Such is the depth of the work of Alfred Hitchcock: It transcends the genre of suspense and shock and makes us consider the human condition. ◉

QUESTIONS

1. What was most likely the author's purpose in writing this passage?
- **A.** to tell the story of Alfred Hitchcock's moviemaking
- **B.** to show why Hitchcock's films are important
- **C.** to show that suspense films are artistic statements
- **D.** to illustrate the technique of point of view

2. According to the passage, which statement is true?
- **A.** Hitchcock liked to surprise and shock audiences.
- **B.** Hitchcock cared little about the technical side of filmmaking.
- **C.** Hitchcock liked to manipulate his audience's emotions.
- **D.** Hitchcock had an optimistic view of human nature.

3. As used in the passage, *voyeur* most nearly means
- **A.** one who watches the actions of others, unseen.
- **B.** a judge of other people's basic human nature.
- **C.** a commentator on the events of a film.
- **D.** a viewer who is expressing non-judgmental opinions.

4. *Rear Window*, *Vertigo*, and *Psycho* are all examples of
- **A.** Hitchcock's relaxed method of filmmaking.
- **B.** films that show Hitchcock's view of human nature.
- **C.** Hitchcock's point of view technique.
- **D.** films that are not challenging for audiences.

5. What would be a more appropriate title for this passage?
- **A.** The Master of Suspense
- **B.** The Filmmaker as Psychologist
- **C.** The Audience as Voyeur
- **D.** Hitchcock: The Master Manipulator

6. *Answer the following question using complete sentences:*
What makes Hitchcock's films more than just suspense stories?

Hedy Lamarr

ONE OF THE MOST BEAUTIFUL actresses of the "Golden Era" of Hollywood during the 1940s and early 1950s was Austrian-born Hedy Lamarr. Despite the celebrity, money, and recognition she achieved during this period, arguably the most interesting aspect of her life had nothing to do with movies, but science.

Few, if any, of the people in movie audiences had an idea that the dazzling beauty they watched onscreen was an accomplished scientist, inventor, and mathematician. Despite the fact that she had left school at the age of 16, and had no further formal education, Lamarr's basic intelligence was such that she was able to absorb complex scientific concepts simply from sitting in on business meetings with her first husband, Friedrich Mandl, an authoritarian Viennese arms manufacturer. Lamarr learned about military technology at these conferences; years later, after she fled her unhappy marriage, she met George Antheil in Hollywood, the man who would become her scientific collaborator. Antheil was an avant-garde composer with a scientific inclination, who had worked out a method for automated control of musical instruments. The two began to develop technology for a secret communication system, which was awarded a patent in 1942. Their invention was an early version of "frequency hopping," in which signals are transmitted by rapidly switching radio waves among many frequency channels, making the signal far less vulnerable to decoding or interference.

Lamarr and Antheil submitted their new technology to the U.S. Navy, seeking support for more research; they believed this was a viable method for making radio-controlled torpedoes. The Navy, however, claimed the invention was too large and heavy to fit into a torpedo, and the concept would lay fallow until 1957, when the Sylvania Electronics Systems Division rediscovered frequency hopping, and began to develop it further.

Ultimately, Sylvania's interest proved to be the **gestation** of the modern secure military communications system. Frequency hopping would also be instrumental in the development of both Internet and cell phone technologies. Fifty-five years after their invention, Lamarr and the since-deceased Antheil were given the Electronic Frontier Foundation Award. When she received it, Hedy Lamarr, screen legend and scientist, tartly responded, "It's about time." ◉

QUESTIONS

1. Based on the passage, what best describes the author's likely purpose in writing it?
- **A.** to explain the concept of frequency hopping
- **B.** to show how Hedy Lamarr helped the war effort
- **C.** to show how Hedy Lamarr was a gifted scientist
- **D.** to show how difficult it is to have two careers simultaneously

2. Based on the passage, which of the following is true?
- **A.** Lamarr had difficulties with the way Hollywood treated her.
- **B.** Lamarr was bored with her acting career.
- **C.** Lamarr and Antheil's invention was a failure because the Navy rejected it.
- **D.** Frequency hopping would lead to many more inventions.

3. Why did the U.S. Navy reject the invention?
- **A.** They didn't believe a Hollywood star could understand science.
- **B.** They didn't think it would ever be small enough to use in a torpedo.
- **C.** Sylvania Electronics already had a patent on it.
- **D.** The Navy already had their own version of the technology.

4. As used in the passage, *gestation* most nearly means
- **A.** the development of an idea.
- **B.** the discarding of an idea.
- **C.** the ridiculing of an idea.
- **D.** the questioning of an idea.

5. Frequency hopping is
- **A.** used to make communication difficult to decode.
- **B.** a method to launch and control torpedoes.
- **C.** a method to communicate via Internet.
- **D.** a mathematical approach to wireless communication.

6. *Answer the following question using complete sentences:*
Would Hedy Lamarr be taken more seriously today as a scientist?

Tin Pan Alley

ACCORDING TO BROADWAY legend, "Tin Pan Alley" got its name from the noise produced by endless piano keys being pounded by composers laboring to create songs to sell to music publishers. Whether this story is truth or legend, in New York City, a street was informally designated as "Tin Pan Alley"—the area on West 28th Street between 5th and 6th Avenues, home to the offices of the major music publishers and the songwriters who worked tirelessly to create hit songs. Before the era of the singer-songwriter, before major stars performed their own work, and before the words of the music changed society, Tin Pan Alley ruled.

The history of this place dates from the late-nineteenth century, when copyright laws protecting the work of songwriters were enacted. Previously, rights for songs had little legal regulations, and competing publishers would sometimes print different versions of the same songs without permission, effectively cheating songwriters out of millions. With the copyright change, composers, lyricists, and publishers began working together for their mutual benefit, and the major music houses established offices in New York City. These offices would become lively networking centers for the **gamut** of entertainment professionals of the period, not only songwriters, but also stars from Broadway and Vaudeville. This was, without a doubt, the beginning of pop music culture, as well as the beginning of promotion for the music industry. Songwriters and publishers used the technique of "song plugging," which meant that instead of waiting for the public to discover the music, they instead brought the songs to the public, by making the rounds of theaters, saloons, cafes, and music halls and getting them performed, one way or another. Many of Broadway's most famous composers and lyricists received their earliest recognition this way, including Irving Berlin, George and Ira Gershwin, Jerome Kern, and Cole Porter, who would all go on to major success on Broadway and in Hollywood.

The end of the Tin Pan Alley era is harder to pinpoint than its beginning; its relevance gradually faded as musical tastes shifted from the ragtime and cakewalk songs of its heyday toward jazz, blues, and eventually rock-and-roll. Nevertheless, its importance to the music industry and American culture will remain crucial, both for its influence in entertainment business practices and for its heritage of great American songs and songwriters. **o**

QUESTIONS

1. **Which of the following best describes the author's probable purpose in writing the passage?**
   - **A.** to explain the shifting tastes in American popular music
   - **B.** to show how numerous songwriters became famous
   - **C.** to give a brief history of a part of American musical history
   - **D.** to show where Tin Pan Alley was located

2. **Copyright laws were important to Tin Pan Alley because**
   - **A.** publishers weren't competing against one another.
   - **B.** songwriters and publishers could work together for their mutual benefit.
   - **C.** composers and publishers were kept from fighting against each other for pay.
   - **D.** making money became easier through enforcement.

3. **"Song plugging" was the process of**
   - **A.** promoting songs by having them performed anywhere possible.
   - **B.** substituting a new song for an old one in a Broadway show.
   - **C.** getting a song copyrighted.
   - **D.** having a well-known star perform a song.

4. **As used in the passage, *gamut* most nearly means**
   - **A.** a series of musical notes.
   - **B.** the full range.
   - **C.** a group.
   - **D.** a union.

5. **The major reason that the Tin Pan Alley era came to an end was that**
   - **A.** ragtime and cakewalk music was banned.
   - **B.** the most successful songwriters moved on to Broadway and Hollywood.
   - **C.** musical tastes shifted.
   - **D.** music publishers moved away from West 28th Street.

6. *Answer the following question using complete sentences:*
   In what ways did Tin Pan Alley point the way toward the contemporary music business?

Insightful and Reader-Friendly, Yet Affordable

Prestwick House Literary Touchstone Classic Editions–
The Editions By Which All Others May Be Judged

Every *Prestwick House Literary Touchstone Classic* is enhanced with Reading Pointers for Sharper Insight to improve comprehension and provide insights that will help students recognize key themes, symbols, and plot complexities. In addition, each title includes a Glossary of the more difficult words and concepts.

For the Shakespeare titles, along with the Reading Pointers and Glossary, we include margin notes and various strategies to understanding the language of Shakespeare.

New titles are constantly being added; call or visit our website for current listing.

Special Introductory Educator's Discount – At Least 50% Off

		Retail Price	Intro. Discount
X200102	Red Badge of Courage, The	$3.99	$1.99
X200163	Romeo and Juliet	$3.99	$1.99
X200074	Heart of Darkness	$3.99	$1.99
X200079	Narrative of the Life of Frederick Douglass	$3.99	$1.99
X200125	Macbeth	$3.99	$1.99
X200053	Adventures of Huckleberry Finn, The	$4.99	$2.49
X200081	Midsummer Night's Dream, A	$3.99	$1.99
X200179	Christmas Carol, A	$3.99	$1.99
X200150	Call of the Wild, The	$3.99	$1.99
X200190	Dr. Jekyll and Mr. Hyde	$3.99	$1.99
X200141	Awakening, The	$3.99	$1.99
X200147	Importance of Being Earnest, The	$3.99	$1.99
X200166	Ethan Frome	$3.99	$1.99
X200146	Julius Caesar	$3.99	$1.99
X200095	Othello	$3.99	$1.99
X200091	Hamlet	$3.99	$1.99
X200231	Taming of the Shrew, The	$3.99	$1.99
X200133	Metamorphosis, The	$3.99	$1.99

PRESTWICK HOUSE, INC.
"Everything for the English Classroom!"

Prestwick House, Inc. • P.O. Box 658, Clayton, DE 19938
Phone (800) 932-4593 • Fax (888) 718-9333 • www.prestwickhouse.com